W9-CRD-875

Also from Telling Our Stories Press

IMPACT: An Anthology of Short Memoirs
SURVIVE: A Collection of Short Memoirs
TURNS: A Collection of Memoir Chapbooks
SO LONG: Short Memoirs of Loss and Remembrance
THE BRIDGE: A Companion Journal for Unearthing
Personal Narratives and Memoir
RESURECTING PROUST: Unearthing Personal
Narratives through Journaling
MY CIA: A Memoir

Praise for
ROLL

"I am delighted by the diversity of voices in ROLL. They are brave and funny, heartbreaking and heartwarming, startling and familiar. Written by people of many ages and backgrounds in forms from traditional narrative to poetry and everything in between, these personal narratives consistently entertain, engage, inspire, and move us. I am grateful to CoCo Harris and the many talented writers of ROLL for giving us their stories."
—Judith Serin, author of *Hiding in the World*

"ROLL...right into intimate and rich stories of people just like you and me. The authors of these stories and poems open their hearts with honest portrayals of significant moments that changed them forever. Your heart will open, too, as you enter in to each remarkable reflection. Savor each selection and feel them nourish your soul."
—Susan Meyn, creator of *JournalCards* and author of *Journal Magic!*
Lessons in Therapeutic Writing

"In ROLL, the narratives and poems flow into cycles of birth, childhood, youth, adulthood and death. These true stories of humanity, cracked and crumbling, wizened by age, disheartened but fighting to thrive, loves lost and loves gained, are polished jewels of eloquent writing on life's excruciating pain and exquisite joy."
—Martha Braniff, author of *Step Over Rio* and
Songs from the Bone Closet

"CoCo Harris knows the value of story. ROLL, her anthology of personal narratives in poetry and prose, gathers together a variety of voices, offering the gift of shared events, experiences and memories that are at once unique and universal. Whether they relate to "Approaching Home," "Redemption," or her other themes, what we realize in reading the included works is that by telling our stories we share our humanity and keep it alive."
—Elayne Clift, author of *Hester's Daughters*

"ROLL: 55 narratives breathed into life by diverse contemporary storytellers. Brave. Raw. Intimate. Moving. This anthology offers truth at every turn. Rich in feeling, profound in insight, these are stories you will remember long after closing the book. Reading them may call up stories of your own, and move you to share them."
—Terry Martin, author of *The Secret Language of Women*

Roll

Roll

A Collection of
Personal Narratives

CoCo Harris

TELLING OUR STORIES PRESS

Telling the Telling Our Stories of Our Lives Press

Showcasing the Art of Literary Personal Narratives

Published by Telling Our Stories Press

The independent literary imprint with a focus on
the art of short memoir and
personal narratives.

Copyright ©2012 by CoCo Harris
All rights reserved.

Library of Congress Control Number: 2011940226

No part of this book may be reproduced or transmitted
in any form or by any means, electronic or mechanical, including photocopying,
recording, or by any information storage and retrieval system without written permission
from the author, except for the inclusion of brief quotations in a review.

Requests for information should be forwarded to:
Telling Our Stories Press
visit
www.TellingOurStoriesPress.com

Cover Art: *How I Roll* by Guinotte Wise, welded steel and found objects
Cover Design: CoCo Harris & Michael Milliken
Book layout: Renee Nixon
UltraShort Memoir™ is a trademark of Telling Our Stories Press
An earlier version of The Tattooed Nurse by Alan Steinberg
appeared in the literary journal Hospital Drive and
is reprinted here with permission from the author.
The quote by E. Ethelbert Miller is taken from *The 5th Inning*
and is reprinted here with permission from the author
and from the publisher, PM Press (www.PMPress.org)

Printed in the United States of America

ISBN-13: 978-0982922859
ISBN-10: 098292285X

For my entire wonderful family,
Mom, siblings, cousins, aunties, uncles,
ancestors and all…

and as always, the O-Girls

and, for Paul Dragavon,
who shared his first memory with us here

"How much do you need to know about death?
It's the memoires of life that bloom into memoir."

—E. Ethelbert Miller, *The 5th Inning*

Acknowledgements

Every piece contained within these pages came from those who somehow heard of the emerging press seeking personal narratives, and shared stories of their lives such that this volume of our collective story can exist. A special thanks to all those on the Telling Our Stories Press Advisory Council, and to all the Galley Reviewers who took the time to graciously provide critical comments, hearty suggestions, necessary edits, assistance, creative encouragement and support. Some of these wonderful folks include George Shields, Nancy Prothro Arbuthnot, and Jude McElroy.

CONTENTS

Open Letter to Us All

I am sitting watching my daughters play at the beach. I am standing in line at DMV renewing my driver's license. I am checking a flight board at the airport confirming my departure time and gate. I'm listening to one of my clients disclosing their invention, and how they came about their discovery. I am waiting at a bus stop.

This is the genesis of how these stories came to me...

Each time that I'm given a piece of our collective story, I think, why did they share this particular story? With me? Be it at random moments along my day, or by way of submissions to an emerging press seeking to make art with short personal narratives, why are these shared with us?

With each narrative, these authors are saying: this is a part of my story— these words embody who I am.

We are telling the stories of our lives:
when we make lists,
when we write letters,
when we recreate dialogue,
when we assemble narrative photography,
when we interpret past experiences
through performance,
and, when we relay our stories through prose and poetry.
This is how we roll—as the cover artist posits.
An ongoing mantra for all Telling Our Stories Press memoir projects is:

"Tell me a story of your life, and
tell me who you are because of it."

This inquiry lies at the heart of all TOSP collections. Within these pages, you will find UltraShort Memoir™ ranging from about 100 words, to longer narratives.

I have always felt that what we tell is as important as how we tell it. I am informed by cultures steeped in traditions of storytelling. I learned from my mom early on "not to listen to what people say—but why they say it." This leads to a deeper level of listening.

So listen.

Listen for the quiet moments of resolve, truth, discovery, healing, revelation…Listen to who we are. Listen to why we are. Listen.

Many voices,

One story,

Ours.

CoCo Harris
Granada, Spain
August 2012

Redux

Joan Goodreau

First Words

"Now Mommy is electrocuting herself," I say as I poke the fork into the toaster to extract the black hard rectangle. The fire alarm shrieks. "Shit. Now Mommy is scraping the toast because this is the last piece of bread in the house." My three kids duck as I sprinkle charred crumbs on their heads.

"Why do you always talk to yourself, Mom?" Mary, my seven year old, asks.

"Shh--shh--it," repeats three-year-old Ian from his high chair.

I stare at him. Maybe it's working. The hospital speech pathologist told me to describe my actions out loud like a voice-over in some educational film we used to watch in school. "Look at Mommy fix coffee. Look at Mommy pour the cereal." All this self-talk pays off. Bathe him with words and eventually Ian will speak even if it's a cuss word.

Ian's word made me rush to the Delayed-Speech Training at the Children's Hospital. Moms and dads sit in rows and face the word wall. Every week, parents write the gurgles, murmurs and grunts of their speech-delayed children on flashcards to put on the Wall. Everyone except me.

"Have you been base lining Ian's words?" chirps the mom beside me. I smile and take the red flash cards for the first time from my bag.

The speech pathologist bounces in dressed in her Winnie-the-Pooh covered scrubs. Winnie and Piglet, even Eeore talk more than our kids do.

"Who has been practicing their self-talk all week?" We all raise our hands like honor students. I cheat. After all-nighters with Ian, I cannot talk to myself before my morning cup of coffee.

"Who wants to post their kid's words?" she asks.

I leap to the wall. This is my first trip, so I want to get a prominent spot. In the past three months, my baseline charts have been empty. Every day is a blank page of Ian's silence. Once I tickled him and wrote down the giggles and tried to spell the sounds of his tantrums. But these are the first sounds he has imitated. I tape three cards "Sh" "sh" "it"--might as well get credit for three.

"Ian's first real word," says the speech pathologist. "Most youngsters don't grasp the abstract concept of 'it.'" I beam while the dads and moms congratulate me. At the end of the meeting, I put on my rain coat and hope for a downpour of Ian's words that will turn into a torrent of talk on which our family can sail back to safe, familiar ground.

Ian doesn't speak again, but I continue to chatter around the house. Any time Mary says something, I repeat it like a parrot, "Good banana, good banana" I yell louder and louder in Ian's face. "GOOD BANANA GOOD BANANA."

Jennifer, my ten-year-old, and her friends say less and less around me because they don't want the human echo machine to start.

"Mom wasn't always like this," she tries to reassure them, but they just stare at her, then me. Jennifer is right. I used to be quiet until I began the parent class six months ago. Then I started to narrate details of our daily lives, and now I sound like a play-by-play announcer of an endless hockey game with no goals.

Ian ignores us and rolls his Hot-Wheels back and forth, back and forth across the table. His eyes fix on the wheels that whir-ir-ir near his ear while "good banana" bounces off the other ear.

"Maybe he just doesn't want to talk." his sisters say.

"I can't shut my brat brother up," Jennifer's friend says, "you're lucky Ian doesn't talk and mouth off to you."

Family legend says my great uncle Herman didn't talk because he couldn't get a word in edgewise with his two older sisters around. The speech pathologist told us "Einstein didn't talk until he was five. Speech would come. It just needed coaxing with some kids."

I wonder, did Einstein reach from his high chair to the pantry and scream while his mother pleaded, "What do you want to eat?"

Ian's sisters yell a duet, "What do you want Ian?" in a game the whole family can play. I hold up peanut butter, cereal, canned pineapple one at a time like a game-show hostess, trying to make each item look like a prize. Ian shakes his wet, red face and reaches his arms even further toward phantom food we cannot see.

This guessing game is simple and can be played anywhere. I guess he wants soup when he reaches toward the can and screams while I heat it. The game is over when Ian shoves his dish of untouched alphabet soup onto the floor. I clean the mess with a dirty mop that looks like Ian's hair, stringy with sweat. I stare at the letters tumbled on the linoleum. All these letters make no words or sense. There is no winner in this game.

I yearn for a quiet dinner hour with Bach playing in the background where we share our day and say please pass the vegetables. We listen to background music every night, all right. Ian varies his pitch, but never his volume. My pediatrician says to ignore his tantrums.

"Pretend they're not happening," he advises.

So my daughters adjust to Ian's syncopations. They hurl peas at each other, kick each other under the table and giggle, while I try to find some food to fill Ian's mouth and stop his heavy metal vocals. Ian's tantrums are sound waves in the air we breathe in and out every day. We take for granted his tantrums the way we do our breath.

I go to the last parent meeting with no new words and face the word wall covered with other children's words. Here are real words of at least three letters: "eat, more, ball, juice, Mommy." Does Ian even know who I am? Am I his Mom or just a hostess offering prizes he doesn't want.

The speech pathologist passes out certificates. "Thank you for your hard work. You have all made progress with your children. They are on their way to being little chatter boxes."

The couples receive their certificates and leave together as if they're going to celebrate at a grad party somewhere. I sit alone, still waiting.

Mrs. Winnie-the-Pooh comes over, holds my hand and says, "I think it's time for further tests."

I try to figure out the meaning of her words. But I cannot understand them any more than I can unscramble the spilled alphabet soup of Ian's wordless code.

Five weeks later, I bring Ian in a stroller to the Imaging department of the hospital. The nurse explains how the Magnetic Resonance Imaging test works while I fill out medical forms.

"The MRI won't take long, and we can take pictures with magnetic field and radio waves to see if there are abnormalities in his brain," she says.

I try to listen at the same time that I write down when Ian walked and talked. He walked the same time as his sister, didn't he? He babbled for his first year then just stopped. Ian's baby book was blank on the "Milestone" pages.

"Don't worry," I used to tell the other moms. "Childhood isn't a race with winners and losers. My kids don't compete with each other. They will all walk to

Kindergarten and talk too much in class."

I tune back to the nurse, "...more accurate than our old CT scans that x-rayed the brain in slices."

I picture Ian's brain like sliced pickled beets.

"He has to lie still on this padded table when he goes into the scanner, so we'll give him a sedative to calm him."

She gives Ian a shot while I hold him on my lap. He wriggles off and circles the MRI tube like a NASCAR racing around the track.

"That shot will soon kick in and settle him down," the nurse says. She attaches straps to the table fours times Ian's length while he still circles.

In a half hour, the doctor orders another shot. Ian sees the nurse coming with the hypo and heads for the door. She calls another nurse to hold his arms while she pokes the needle in. Ian screams and kicks her in the stomach.

"Don't worry, he'll calm down after this," the nurse reassures me, rubbing her abdomen.

I always did what the doctor ordered and took medicine my mother gave me. It might taste bad, but it cured you. So when Ian arches his body and two nurses hold him down, I think it is for his own good. This is an easy test to show if there is something wrong. I try to hold him on my lap again, but he lurches, falls to the floor and rolls back and forth.

A half hour later, another nurse comes in to say we're behind schedule. The doctor comes in and says, "I don't know why the sedative's not working because we gave him enough to down an elephant. Let's give it a go anyway."

Two nurses grab Ian by his arms and legs, press him on the table and strap his head, chest and arms. Ian bellows like an elephant that is not sedated, but wounded. He starts to choke and sprays the nurses with spit and snot.

The machine grinds and the table creeps into the tube like the car-wash tunnel which scares Ian so much our car is always dirty. I cannot move, as if I too were strapped down. I watch a show I cannot stop or leave.

Ian curls his body against the straps and looks at me before his head disappears. The tube devours his shoulders and arms. Only his feet and pants, drenched with pee, remain in sight. Suddenly the screaming stops, and I listen to the fan buzzing inside the machine. Has he stopped breathing? The doctor and the nurses stand still.

"Let me out of here." His voice comes clear and loud from the dark tunnel. "Let me out."

I leap from my chair, stare at the tube and listen to the stranger's voice. "Those are his first words, his first words."

Taps and clicks from the magnetic cameras signal that the test is over. Ian slides out and stares at the ceiling. I lift his stiff body and put him back in the stroller. He does not look at me.

Ian falls asleep in his car seat on the ride back home because the sedative finally kicks in. I grab the steering wheel to stop my hands from shaking and creep along the Freeway as if in heavy fog, even though the sun is shining. Just get home to safety, I tell myself, as I exit.

I carry him upstairs to bed and clutch the banister to steady my legs. I rock him, still asleep, and look down at his smooth head and mop hair. Magnetic waves and radio pulses of energy took pictures of the size and shape of his brain, but I don't care what he looks like inside. No more torture. We're just going to get along with the way he is.

The girls come back from school while I watch Ian sleep in his crib. So I go downstairs to the kitchen and put out corn flakes and milk in two bowls.

"Eat, get in your pajamas, go to bed."

"We just got home Mom. We have homework," says Jennifer.

"Eat, get in your pajamas, go to bed."

"But it's light outside; the kids are playing," Mary whines.

Then Jennifer tells her, "It's okay. Mom's off again today. We'll wait until she goes upstairs and then find the Halloween candy she hid."

Their words follow me to my bedroom. I close the drapes, lie in the dark and wrap the quilt around me, a tube so tight I hardly breathe.

"Let me out of here," I whisper.

Kent H. Dixon

In Reply to Your Last Suicide Note

In reply to your last suicide note, I must say that even with the "legitimate objects of matrimony" as the documents phrased it, even with them long gone since, it hurt me terribly to see them slapping your face and calling your name, jamming those tubes down your handsome throat while loudly demanding your birthday.

—She never knows her birthday, I said.

—Who's this guy? From an orderly

—Wait outside, please, sir? The preemptory nurse

I didn't try to cover you, what would be the point? Who besides me could know how much more than barest tit lay exposed there, except him, little whathisname as you preferred to call him, even as you held him to it, your breast.

—Like sucking boils with hard little gums, you said. You knew.

When you snarfed down those pills, you knew I'd be off early and he's be the next to stir, spilling a trail of stuffed animals from his bed to yours, to climb in and snuggle; you knew; you knew you'd be dead by then.

But he would have to have waited for me to come home for dinner to read him your thoughtful note. Didn't you worry he'd catch cold, bundling all day with corpse?

Well, he's in school now and has learned his P's and Q's, is quick to recognize his Bull Winkles and Daba-daba-doos on the supermarket shelf, and elsewhere. Just last week this remaining object of matrimony, little whatthefuck I say, took an overdose of vitamin pills, in order, he said, to make himself sick, like mommy.

Tiffany Joy Butler

Doodle On

A chandelier hangs in the dining room of my childhood home. The dining table is newly bought by Mom's obsession with shopping. The table's legs are columns with a history of the Greek or Roman past. I'm not Greek or Roman. A glass pig is hollow to fit all our pennies in. A bright pink dollhouse with bright pink dolly dresses is in the back of me. There are porcelain dolls on top of the China cabinet; Mom collects dolls, knick-knacks, and plates. I'm sitting across from Dad, my feet barely touching the floor. I'm so small. Daddy is eating frosty flakes. I'm just sitting.

I look into the cabinet; the distraction of pretty white dolls. Dad has a brown afro, but on the middle of his head, the hair is starting to fade. Today, he is unusually quiet. But he's such a talker, especially to strangers. He talks to me about goodness, to be a good student, a good person, to be polite, to think before I act. At the age of eight, I am the best citizen. I am a good student, and a good little Christian girl who prays every night.

"Remember to give God thanks," he says.

Right before I say goodbye to the moon without ever questioning what it means to pray or be grateful, I thank God for all that I had- the Barbie dolls, the health of the family, etc. I pray that he continues the blessings of the physical objects, the physical presence of things.

At the dining table that we rarely use after this moment, his face looks worn out now like an overused tire. His leather jacket is dangling off the chair next to him. His hands, they carry cracks and scars. They are open wounds. They are dry with the taste of car oils. I stare at him. He is funny. He is my clown.

"Piggy back! Piggy back!" I plea.

On numerous occasions, Dad would say, "Yes." He'd pretend to be a pig for a while. He is so good at it- he'd snort just like a pig! Holding on tight, he'd give me a lively ride throughout the house.

"No, not right now. I have something to tell you."

Daddy puts down his spoon as if he finishes his meal in a jiffy. He flips his tan leather jacket on; he has one of the best styles in clothes.

"Daddy? Where you going?"

Even before my birth, Dad worked in the used car business. Unlike most, he learned to read through newspapers and not through schooling.

He tugs at his tan leather jacket. He looks at me. I look back at him.

"Daddy? Are you coming back soon?"

"I have to go, Kiddo."

I run to his body and hug him. I hold tight to his strong brown legs.

Dad went to jail for eight months, but the family lie was he went to help his sick mother. Shortly after, Mom filed bankruptcy. The pennies in the glass piggy bank dwindled, and the dolls weren't as important as the letters I wrote to him.

The day after he left, I drew a picture of Dad holding my hand. Brown squiggly lines equaled our hair, tan squares equaled our bodies, and blue rectangles equaled our legs. The sun was a yellow-orange circle smiling and the grass was greener than real life.

Sandra Branum

Eye Fear

Searing pain engulfs me as I struggle to stop the pounding in my chest and the flowing tears that laugh at my feeble stop attempts. I reach for the wine because I *KNOW* this will stop the vicious cycle by either causing me to sleep or get me drunk. At this moment, either one will do. *I can't hold on anymore.* You see tomorrow I face another eye shot, and just can't take it anymore, but what else can I do if I want to see? My eyes know this, and so they mock me!

Marian Rapoport

Healing

A lovely sensuous shell. Curved with a delicate kind of bone structure. I'm reminded of the inner ear and smile, thinking of how children are taught early on to hold conch shells up to their ears, to listen to the sound of the waves.

Perfectly drawn spirals of energy, of motion centering at a point that protrudes like a nipple on a soft flesh-toned breast.

Grains of fine sand hide within the bony folds of the dim interior. Something has lived within, grown safely within. And all that's left is the sandy droppings of the shoreline that tell us something about where this creature once settled down into home.

I'm with Ally, my German Shepherd, who's living with cancer, teaching me in these remaining months of her life to also live with cancer and maybe even to thrive on it. We comb the empty vast beaches on many a chilly spring day. I'm obsessed with these particular shells. I find them everywhere, stuffing my sweatshirt pockets with them, filling my jean jacket too. At first, I pick even the ones with broken pieces. Maybe especially the ones with broken pieces. Then on an outing later that same month, I want only the shells that seem whole. I find many and take them home.

I didn't know shells could be so female. I see the breast in all her soft supple round beauty. I see an eye in the center of the shell, which is also a nipple. And the road leading to it winds like a spiral staircase that goes round and round with ends becoming new beginnings and energy circling on and on.

That was in the springtime some years ago. It's take me until now to understand that those shells and the ones I still collect keep healing me from my own brokenness at the time, my breast cancer, that deep down abiding hurt within.

Ann Marie Byrd and Janet Youngblood

I Faced the Challenge

"Lieutenant Stilt, they really need you badly at Fort Benning, Georgia, at the infantry school. With your experience and skills, and with all this training, they are eager to have you there."

I thought they looked forward to having me and needed me badly. So I went, all flags flying, down to Fort Benning. Reported for duty to the adjutant. Direct! Oh my God. He told me they were not expecting me and they didn't want me. They didn't know what to do with me. I was a First Lieutenant with lots of rank, and if they took me in they would keep one of their male Second Lieutenants from a promotion. So I was about as welcome as . . . you name it.

We were out in the sticks and they had no place to put me. They trained male infantry officers, the "Ninety Day Wonders," away from the main post, out in the wilds because they needed lots of space for the firing range and the three-month training they had to go through. For my first three days I sat and wrote personal letters. They didn't know what to do with me. Finally they decided they were stuck with me and put me across the road in the personnel office, reporting to that same male Second Lieutenant who resented me 100 percent plus. I was keeping him from getting a promotion.

I was his superior officer but that didn't make any difference. I was a woman. Army ground forces were notorious for being the last to accept women as equals. The old foot soldiers, the ones with the bayonets, they faced the enemy one-on-one. They were the last to admit we could do anything. There again, I faced the challenge.

A company of WACs [Women's Army Corps] stayed on the main post and although I wasn't a part of their group, I used their facilities. I left the base to go work every day. At some point I had a jeep and a driver taking me back and forth.

The United States didn't want any part of Europe's war. We were isolationist because we had fought in World War I, the war to end all wars, and we didn't want another. Let them fight it out. When the Japanese attacked Pearl Harbor, December 7, 1941, I was in Phoenix that Sunday morning. I had come down for breakfast. We heard the announcement on the radio. *Where is Pearl Harbor?* We didn't know where that was. But that marked the turning point. Patriotism led me to enlist. Born in 1918—World War I—it may have been something abut that. I wanted to do what I could and I knew I had some very valuable skills—expert typing, expert stenographer, expert office skills.

Originally the Women's Army Auxiliary Corps recruited volunteers for officer candidates. Although I wanted to go, I did not apply because of family reasons. Then circumstances changed and I felt I was able to go. It just happened that the Army wanted volunteers for the initial cadre, the very first group to go into basic training as noncommissioned officers. The others in that first group, from all over the country, were officer candidates.

We went by train from Phoenix to Fort Des Moines, spending a couple nights in the Pullmans. I was with a group from Phoenix, about twenty, most of them officer candidates. Betty Bandel, whose letters appeared in *An Officer and a Lady[1]*, was in that group.

I didn't apply to the Corps until after they had closed applications for officers. The recruiting officer said, "Why didn't you come in earlier? You scored higher than most of the officer candidates." I said, "It was a personal reason, so I couldn't." I went in rank from private to captain, not that fast, but pretty fast.

The telephone company in Phoenix gave me a leave of absence for military service. That's what changed my mind about going in. They granted leaves of absence for military service for men going into service—jobs were guaranteed on return, with all their service credit. The company felt that it was only fair to offer women a leave of absence. Well, that did it for me, because I'm security minded. They had a plan so that for the first three months of your military service they would make up the difference between your job pay and your military pay. So for three months they gave me the difference between my $21 and whatever I was making. That enabled me to feel I wasn't deserting the family. By then they were growing up and getting jobs, so I wasn't leaving them high and dry. But the financial incentive did it.

The only one I talked to about enlisting was my mother. At twenty-four I knew I didn't need her permission, but I wanted her blessing. I told her I wanted to do this and she said some wonderful words to me, about how I had earned it. She was glad her only boy was too young to go and her eldest wanted to go. I had earned the right to do it. Words of wisdom. See, I gave up college to support the family. I had lots of responsibility for many years. My mother said, "Maybe this will be a substitute for your having to give up college." I was the ultimate student—wanted to be a Latin teacher. I started seventh grade at Walnut Hills High School in Cincinnati, the ultimate for college prep, and a very selective public school. All my classmates went to Vassar and Wellesley and I thought I'd be among them.

I knew I would be talked out of my decision because I was the ultimate, feminine lady—always wore white, always immaculate, always beautifully groomed. Very sheltered as far as many things in life were concerned. Old fashioned—Ohio Corn Belt—values.

I had mixed feelings on the train. I never lived away from home before and I hadn't told a soul until I took the oath. People tried to talk me out of it

---

[1] *An Officer and a Lady: The World War II Letters of Lt. Col. Betty Bandel, Women's Army Corps,* edited by Sylvia J. Bugbee, 2004.

but it was too late. In fact, when I got my letters of recommendation from my employer, I didn't say it was the Army because I was keeping it secret. My employer thought I was looking for another job but I had already taken the oath. An executive said, "Why didn't you tell us that you wanted more money?"

I arrived in Des Moines, July 20, 1942, the first day that WAACs came to the Fort. The newspaper devoted pages to our arrival. Lots and lots of pictures. One newspaper reporter had me get back on the steps of the train and pose. I pretended to wave at someone so he could take my picture. Of course, there was something in the paper about the Battle of Stalingrad in there, another turning point in the war.

They transported us by truck to the Fort. For some reason I rode up in front with the driver. Well, as I say, the ultimate feminine: the Stafford shoes, the polka-dot peplum, the off-the-face white pique hat—

Basic training. Oh my God. My whole family, we were night owls, and getting up in the morning was always a problem. I had to do it at the Fort, of course, but I had no idea what it would be like to have a whistle blowing and lights in my eyes at an early hour. So many people, no privacy, but I adapted pretty quickly. There was no alternative. I looked at those narrow cots and thought I'd fall off the bed but I didn't because I'd be exhausted. The worst part was getting so much done so early. You'd get up, get ready—you had to do your space, march to breakfast. It was like doing a full day's work before you marched off to class. By 7:30.

We were in big brick buildings, two and three stories high, by the Parade Ground. I think they were previously officers' quarters. The officer candidates and enlisted women stayed in similar buildings, all in the same row. We had the same accommodations as they had. Don't forget, there weren't very many of us.

Of necessity, men trained us. The enlisted men and officers were all men. That was an experience. For formation, for reveille, we had a very hard-boiled, old, regular Army sergeant. He had been told to clean up his language. He was in total frustration when he talked to us, trying to keep his language polite. His name was Paine—Sergeant Paine. He pretty much succeeded, but he'd get red in the face from trying so hard.

As a member of that first group, I saw that the men were not used to having women in the Army. Talk about resentment. When I picked up my sheets, I heard it from my supply sergeant. I'm young and flip, and said, "What's the matter sergeant? Don't you like having women in your Army?" Oh boy. "A woman's place is in the home." He slammed those sheets down.

The Army tried to prepare for women and did an awfully good job up to a point. They ran out of toilet paper. Women use more toilet paper than men do. Sergeant Paine announced at formation that we would be limited to four sheets of toilet paper per day. Four little squares of toilet paper a day. We stood at attention in ranks, but the minute we left—*Are you kidding?* We kept on using the paper—we tried to be sparing with it—but no way can you get by with four little squares per day.

They still had urinals in those buildings. I thought they were for washing our galoshes. I didn't know. I'd never been in a men's room before. I said, "Wasn't it thoughtful of them to put these in so we can wash our galoshes?" The others must have thought I was the greenest pea they'd ever seen.

When we were first allowed off the post in Des Moines, to go into town, civilians looked upon as an oddity or a novelty. As taxpayers, felt they had every right to come up and feel the sleeves of our uniforms.

After basic training I worked as a stenographer for the male officers instructing the WAAC officer candidates. I typed lessons and they were favorably impressed. I really had a lot of skill. The men in charge of setting up the second WAAC training center sent me to Daytona Beach, Florida, to help organize headquarters. I set up the file system and handled paperwork. It was quite responsible for a private. We went down in October or November 1942.

The Army took over lovely hotels right on the beach. I think it was the Clarendon Hotel—*This is for me!* This is my style of living. Chandeliers and carpets and nice furniture. Someone asked one of the incoming recruits to clean the latrines and she didn't know what a latrine was. She thought they meant the chandeliers in the hotel. I wasn't there very long but of course they removed the carpeting and the chandeliers and we had to scrub everything. And I remember the insects. They were everywhere. With my fair skin, I was a target for mosquitoes.

All of a sudden I received orders to go to OC School in Fort Des Moines. I was picked to be part of the very first group of officers chosen from the ranks. I always seemed to be in the first group to do things. All my life. I don't know why. I think I like challenges.

I headed back to Des Moines. Here I thought I was set for the winter in Florida but I wound up at Fort Des Moines, falling on the ice. I was in OC School, back on Parade Row. We felt sorry for ourselves at Christmas time because we weren't able to go home. Somebody had this bright idea. We had never done KP. So we volunteered to relieve the WAACs on KP. I had pots and pans—those big greasy pots. The WAACs were overwhelmed that officer candidates came in and gave them a day off. It made us feel *so* good. We were exhausted afterwards, took our showers, and went to the Post theatre to reward ourselves. It was a nice thing to do. Instead of feeling sorry for ourselves we went over there and got into the pots and pans. That was my only KP experience and I volunteered for it.

The first women officers were called Third Officer, Second Officer, and First Officer but they were the equivalent of Second Lieutenant, First Lieutenant, and Captain. This is '42, so I'm dealing with male officers, but I'm also working with women officers who have just been commissioned.

Brand new Third Officers, brand new Second Lieutenants. There wasn't time yet for them to be anything higher than that.

I was commissioned in January. That's when I went to the Hotel Savery downtown because the Army had taken over some of the hotel. I wasn't there very long before they asked me to help open the third training center at Fort Oglethorpe, Georgia. The WAACs had been successful despite all the predictions. We had forts at Des Moines, Daytona Beach, and now Fort Oglethorpe.

I was in personnel and, this sounds ghastly, in charge of the section where we terminated people. Those who didn't behave well, and the paperwork involved in that. It was easy to get terminated if you disgraced the Corps. You had to be a lady. If an enlisted woman went out with an officer, she might not be terminated, but she'd certainly be called upon the carpet. WAACs were not allowed to get married. If you got married, you would be out of the service. That'd be one way to get out, I guess. But it could take you from the frying pan into the fire.

Our mission as a Corps was to replace men so they could go into combat. Take over the so-called cushy jobs that women could do. I was at Oglethorpe long enough to become a First Lieutenant, about a year, before becoming one of the first women to attend the Adjutant General's School at Fort Meade, Maryland, one of eight women in a big class of male officers. The school trained officers to become specialists in the Adjutant General field. They run the headquarters. In the Army a regimental adjutant is a captain.

I finished this AG course and received orders to go into the field. I had only worked at WAAC training centers before this, handling administrative work. Now I'm going out into the real Army world at Fort Benning—not just in that particular job that I mentioned in the beginning—until the end of the war.

I started out with that Second Lieutenant, remember. Part of that time I reported to a warrant officer who wasn't even an officer. It was horrible. The Second Lieutenant eventually received another job assignment. Our commanding officer was a West Point colonel and gave me superior—not just outstanding—performance reviews. They realized they had somebody who could do something. My performance opened their eyes to my ability. Later I became regimental adjutant, captain, and ran the officer candidate school for men. It was a big responsibility.

I was in personnel at Fort Benning infantry OC School before I became Adjutant. I'll get emotional talking about it, but I'm very proud. The Army would say, "In addition to other duties you are appointed to do this or that." One of my assignments was the most responsible job I ever had in my life. Why they let a First Lieutenant do this, I do not know. I took it so seriously that I almost had a breakdown. In the OC School, the men underwent a thirty-day review, a sixty-day review, and received their commissions after ninety days. If a man washed out after the thirty-day review, he was out. Or the sixty-day review. Any man who washed out from that OC School was subject to a policy called POR, Personnel for Overseas Replacement. My job required me to sign a "yes" or "no" that that individual is qualified to be sent immediately to a port of embarkation to replace someone lost in combat overseas.

Not just initials. Sign my name. Granted, I was given a checklist of things the men had to complete satisfactorily. I took it so seriously. I wanted to be sure when I signed my name that every "t" had been crossed and every "i" had been dotted. That the men met certain qualifications. I had all these records coming into me, their marksmanship records, their health records, all the different requirements to be considered before sending them overseas. They had already washed out. They were not making it as an officer. But before the Army sent them any place else, the men had to go through this screening process by me. I didn't see them. Don't misunderstand. I had their records.

It was interesting from the human standpoint to see the various reactions. You can argue whether that was a fair thing to do or not. People have said, *Well they were just like other ordinary guys. Why should they get special attention?* But here they are, these young men, they've not made it as officer candidates and they're immediately sent overseas to combat, no leave, nothing. Some of the parents would get in touch with their congressmen to try to stop this. We had some who pretended to be mentally ill, psychoneurotic. But every man who shipped out had to qualify on all scores.

I'm still in my twenties, a young girl, a First Lieutenant. That was a tremendous responsibility. I would say, "Yes, he's qualified," and they would cut the orders. I didn't hand these guys their overseas orders. The sergeant did. They would come in and get their orders. I saw them come in. The fellow I was dating used to say, "Janet, this is all very dignified and businesslike and military. Then you see these fellows come in and you head for the ladies room and cry." That was pretty much the truth.

Some of them were so brave. Handsome young men, and for some reason they didn't cut it for officer training, and they were going to the port of embarkation. This was in preparation for D-Day. It was part of the job. I have no idea how many went over there that didn't come back.

Thank God I don't know.

I only know that I worked so hard. I evidently did such a superlative job that the people at the point of embarkation wrote a letter through the lines of organization to the powers-that-be at Fort Benning. It was a commendation for the superlative work done at Fort Benning on this particular assignment. No exceptions. They found nothing wrong with anything I sent them.

I think having had a lot of responsibility as a child helped me. Remember, I was the oldest in my family and a serious kid. I had to be the example to the other four. I don't know how you feel about the lineup of kids, but I can almost tell you who was an oldest child. They were instilled a sense of responsibility. With my mother ill and my having to work during the

Depression and go to school at the same time, I didn't have much of a youth. I'm making up for it now. They call me the party girl—at ninety!

I was at Fort Benning, Georgia, when President Roosevelt died at Warm Springs. In the hospital. The Army took my tonsils out and that very day Franklin Roosevelt died. That's why I remember the date. He was our hero. Regardless of politics, having lived through this horrible Depression, he gave the country hope. I don't think things today can get as bad as back then because we have brakes in place. I definitely feel that Barack Obama can lead the country. I just feel the man has these old fashioned values and I feel that those are the values that have stood the test of time. Such as basic fairness and honesty.

VJ Day, that was something else again. Fort Benning was a huge post, like a small city. By then I had a lovely apartment on the main post and a jeep driver to take me back and forth to the office. I worked very hard, but remember, I'm a young, attractive girl with all these men. I enjoyed my time at Fort Benning from that standpoint. When the war came to an end we were all thrilled. But regardless of your rank, not one person was allowed to leave the post that night for the little town of Columbus, outside Fort Benning. Even if you were a colonel, you could not leave because they didn't want us to take over that little town and rip it to pieces with celebrations. So we went from one officer's house to another with parties all night long. I remember my date saying, "Janet, these people want to go home." "Oh, they do?" "These people want to go to bed, Janet." "They do?" That was a big night.

I was a returning veteran, a woman captain. In those days that was still rather rare, kind of special. Young and fairly attractive, I had my choice of jobs. I took the one that I didn't think I would have chosen. I had never been to San Francisco but I knew I wanted to live there. I looked at the map to see where they had separation centers. You had about three days at a separation center while they did all the paperwork to get you out of the service. I said, "What is the nearest one to San Francisco?" Camp Beale, Marysville. I wrote my orders to be relieved from active duty at Camp Beale, Marysville, forwarding address General Delivery, San Francisco. So sight unseen—that was another smart decision.

Three-and-a-half years in the Army—I've never felt they owed me a thing. I got so much out of that service. It's amazing what you can do when you have to do things. My family had instilled a sense of confidence in me. I was always expected to be the best and had to live up to that, or try to be. The Army strengthened my sense of confidence.

They asked me to remain. At the separation center I ran into a lieutenant colonel that had been at Fort Benning. He begged me to stay in. He'd give me another promotion. I said, "No. I want to be a civilian now. The war is over." Then we were asked to join the reserve. I didn't because they said, "All you have to do is go to the Presidio a couple weekends a month." I said, "No. I want to be a civilian. I want to wear pretty clothes. I want to get an apartment all my own and I want to learn to cook."

I got to San Francisco and bought two books: *First Steps in Cooking*, a basic, elementary cookbook. I said, "I want a book that tells me how I will know when water is boiling." I also bought *The Bartender's Guide* because I thought if I know how to make a good drink, they won't care what they're eating. I got myself a little apartment, entertained, and had a wonderful time. And I got a husband or two. I was the mother to my sisters and brother, who became a career Air Force man. He served in three wars.

I'd like to be remembered, here's a worn-out phrase, as someone who's made a difference. I know I made a big difference in the Army. A number of people have said I'm their role model, although I don't know that I have earned this. It was not just the Army. I've survived four cancer surgeries, so I don't think we can give the Army credit for that. No. I think all the things I've gone through have made me stronger. I'm very strong. It may sound a bit corny, but I feel every challenge made me stronger for the next one. Like spiritual muscle. I have my down days, but at ninety-two there's an awful lot I can still do.

Gabrijel Savic Ra

On The March 9th I Lost My Youth

It was March 9th, 1991. I was thirteen years old. The Bosnian war started and people were filling the streets to protest. For as long as I have known myself, I never believed in violence of any kind. But, I had to go to the protest. I couldn't be at home knowing that someone like my father was being shot; someone like my mother being raped; or someone like my brother being slaughtered. I was at home with my two grandmothers. My parents were visiting my sick aunt and my brother was hiding at his friend's house, so they wouldn't take him to war.

I told my grandmothers I was going to my best friend's house and that I would return in the
    evening.

I was on the bus and I could hear people murmuring, but I didn't understand what they were saying.

Presence was no longer a homogeneous time-determination, but the moral imperative of awareness of what makes us the creatures that need compassion.
    Youthful enthusiasm bears impulse to go further, or digression of everything...because the intellect can accept only certain structures that lead to absolutely nothing.

I was snapped away from thinking with all people leaving the bus, and I realized that I was at my stop.

I was walking slowly.

I arrived on the main square in Belgrade where there were so many people yelling. I tried to get closer to where I would see the speakers. People were listening to them, then applauding and yelling.

Then, I heard shots. People were screaming. I was not tall enough so I couldn't see all that was happening. Suddenly, something covered my face and jacket. I saw red and white pieces.
    When I looked up, I saw a young man, maybe in his mid-twenties. He had long hair and half of his jaw was missing. His eyes wide open, no tears, just a big hole where once his jaw was. His was shot by a rubber bullet. People surrounded him and were holding him as they took him away.

"Protect the child, take him out of here," they started yelling. Than I realized that they were referring to me. Two older men took me by the arms and lifted me away from there. I was silent. They wiped the blood from my face and my jacket. The jacket I had for many years. I eventually burned it.

They took me to the bus stop and made sure I got on. I got home, went to my room, took off my clothes off, took a bath and went to bed.

I didn't want to wake up, but I did. I had the same body, but I was now a hundred years old.

Choose Your Way to Be Forgotten

(photo by Srdjan Veljovic)

SPOT Festival of Autoperformance
Belgrade, Serbia 2009

Erica Herd

Terror

It is 1987. She is wearing a housedress and zoris, chasing me with scissors out of my Bronx basement apartment and into the elevator. The elevator door slams shut and she stands there screaming, veins popping out of her petite, yet muscular, arms. She said it was her apartment and that my boyfriend had to leave. That she was staying put. She always had trouble with boundaries. In September, she moved into a women's shelter on the Upper East Side. I was a student at Hunter College. She visited me in the afternoon and we'd have coffee in Styrofoam cups in the lobby café. I was afraid someone would figure out she was homeless, that she'd cause a scene. But she didn't. She told me she went there on her own sometimes for coffee. It was the highlight of her day. She lived in the shelter for six months and found an apartment in the Bronx near Bill and me.

I want the terror to stop. I want her out of my head and my heart. How do I accomplish that? She used to call me "the great stone face" because of my calm in the face of crisis and adversity.

She found it amusing, but I didn't.

Alan L. Steinberg

The Tattooed Nurse

"Beauty is in the eye of the beholder."

A cliché is just a cliché until you've lived it, I guess. Then it becomes life. Your life. My life. Words get transformed into joy or sorrow or regret; into tears or laughter; into the faces and voices and images that fill our dreams or nightmares. In a way, then, it's like our lives are a long journey through a land of old sayings. If we're lucky, we'll get to live out mostly the good ones (*Laughter is the best medicine*), or the ones that teach us and strengthen us and console us without leading to disaster (*It is better to have loved and lost than never to have loved at all*).

The birth of a child takes us deep into the forest of clichés: "*The miracle of life,*" "*In sorrow thou shalt bring forth children,*" and the one that taught me the most about human life - something sad and beautiful, both - "*Beauty is in the eye of the beholder.*" When my daughter was born, or was trying to be born, I was lost in the very heart of the cliché woods - right there in the "birthing room," doing the full Lamaze, as it were, sharing in the "great miracle of life." Twenty hours of premature contractions and false labor and deep breathing gave an existential truth to the words "labor of love" and to God's original Biblical curse, "In sorrow thou shalt bring forth children." Hour after hour of "OK, push, push, good, good. Now breathe, breathe," in a sterile room with ghost-white walls and piercing fluorescent lights leaves little time for joyful contemplation. Add to that, the mother-to-be strapped and harnessed to a metal chair-bed like something the Marquis de Sade might have invented, while the father-to-be alternately sits beside her or paces up and down like a devoted coach cheering on a losing team, and the extent of God's punishment becomes clearer. And that's before you begin to factor in the cost of that giving birth and then raising a child in this dangerous and uncertain world. So, it's not surprising that after that first full working day of "hard labor," the wonder and joy and togetherness had grown weary and stale. And the confident and cheerful, "Push, push, breathe, breathe" had become instead, "Push, goddammit, push" and "You push, you bastard."

There were a hundred other clichés we elbowed our way past on that day of "false" or "extended" or "protracted" labor: all the "No pain. No Gain," "When the going gets tough, the tough get going," little inanities that had seemed so much more substantial the evening before. Only once, during one of those blessed "contraction cessation" periods, did I even begin thinking about the baby itself, or herself, my daughter. We knew it was a she because some months before, by the "miracle of modern technology," we had seen the somagraphic image of her, hairless and seal-like, floating tranquilly in that primordial inner sea, tethered by the umbilical cord like an astronaut floating in space. What must she be thinking, seeing, feeling, I thought fleetingly: light at the end of the tunnel, the whole world shaking and trembling like a massive earthquake? What would she make of the sudden draining of that warm and secure belly-pond, as the nurse with a weary and hollow optimism had called out, "Her waters have broken. It won't be long now" - converting the medicinal, "the amniotic sac has torn" into the more Biblical-sounding expression. No wonder all our human lives we live in uneasy fear of the dark, of tomorrow, of salvation. We're born in a storm and live out our lives awaiting the next one.

But all the horror of the labor and delivery pales in the actual presence of "the delivered." Nothing in the greeting card, saccharine sentimentality of expressions like "new life," "the baby," or the "precious little one," prepares you for the grotesque, slimy, misshapen ugliness of what actually emerges into that unforgiving white light. Anyone who still can't believe we're descended from apes needs only to be there, right there, in "the birthing room." A giant, hairy, wrinkled, slime-coated, dented head atop bowl-legged dwarf-legs doesn't even begin to suggest the simian - no, the extraterrestrial - appearance of a human infant. Twenty hours of push and breathe, of waters breaking and blood flowing and then this: something Hieronymus Bosch might have sketched on a particularly troubled night.

The nurse, whatever she was thinking, held the pumpkin-headed ball of hair and slime up to me and said (the way a decapitated person might say, if the head could still speak, "Well, at least they left my body alone"): "Who does she look like?"

"I can't speak for her family," I said, barely able to look at the woman nearly passed out and quietly sobbing below me, the thing's mother, "but we don't have any orangutans in mine."

The nurse seemed genuinely shocked for an instant, but then managed a brittle little chuckle, the way we do when we've just heard a lame joke we don't quite get or don't want to. But I tell you I didn't really mean it as a joke. In fact, for a brief moment in time I was thinking of the possibility of alien impregnation - the kind you get in the B-horror films. I even began trying to think back nine months: had I gone out of town? had anything odd happened in the house, the yard, the nearby woods? Had there been any UFO-type sightings reported in the news?

"We need to go to the Obstet Lab," the nurse said brightly, breaking my frantic efforts at recall. She was holding "the baby" up to me, now wrapped in some white towel-like cloth, and cradling its slender, rubbery neck with her palm. "You want to carry her?" she asked, with the forced cheerfulness of someone holding a ticking time-bomb.

"No, that's all right," I blurted out, aghast at the thought of holding whatever it was she was holding.

The nurse gave me a sharp look - one bordering on anger or disgust or bewilderment. The old conspiracy of women, I thought. 'We know that half the genes are ours; we carried it. But you'll never know for certain, will you?' And right then it hit me: I had been out-of-town nine months ago. Gone for a week. On business. Perhaps they had been watching from a distant ship, waiting their chance. A kind of Martian version of Rosemary's Baby. One-by-one, plant the seed. Wait until they had grown. Let the poor dumb human raise the thing as his own. Bear all the misery and expense. And then one day have the mutants rise up and take over the world - prepare it for the full invasion. Hadn't they made a movie about it already?

I was thinking all these thoughts as we walked slowly out of "the birthing room" into the long corridor that would take us to the Obstetrics Lab, to the "Preparation Room," where, the nurse chattered on, they would weigh her and measure her and put the silver nitrite in her eyes, or some such thing. I barely heard. I was thinking that here, surely, in the Preparation Room, the horrible truth would emerge. The nurse there would see something alien. Would sound the alarm. The police would be called. The FBI. The Men-in-Black. Will Smith himself. There would be questioning. Torture. Truth serum.

"I have to go now. Here. You hold her like this and then turn left at the end of the corridor. The nurse will be waiting for you," a voice said, again breaking my reverie.

And then I felt the weight of something in my arms, something alive and breathing and moving. Something somehow mine. The sudden weight of her in my arms, the physicality, the gravitational pull - all combined in that instant to turn the abstraction, the "it," "the alien," into my daughter - for all her simian appearance. If the mother ship came for her now, they'd have a fight on their hands. They'd see what human resistance and courage and devotion were all about. And just as I was thinking all this, I came to the end of the corridor and turned towards the Obstetrics Lab. And my heart froze.

Standing in the narrow hallway, directly before the open door of the Preparation Room, his head nearly scraping the sign protruding from the top of the door frame, was a man dressed all in hospital white, like an orderly, except the sleeves had been cut off at the shoulders to reveal two massively muscled arms crisscrossed with dozens of terrifying tattoo-shapes: death-heads, and jungle-animals, and coiled snakes. He was maybe six-three or four, with thick, shiny, flat-topped hair and a long, handle-bar mustache - mostly black but with some streaks of grey that made me realize he must be early middle-age, maybe in his forties. And yes, I knew right away that he was a Hell's Angel biker, and that he would try and snatch my daughter from me and run off with her to sell on the black market. I'd read in the paper not long before about some such thing - a market for healthy Caucasian babies for the rich and sterile or foreign. It all came together in an instant - the man, the tattoos, the wide-eyed drug-crazed grin. He would grab her, race down the hall, jump on his motorcycle and take off with her. Somewhere down the road there'd be a van waiting. He'd hand her to the driver, get his wad of money, slip out of the hospital clothes back into his jeans and black jacket and be just one more hog-riding bad-ass heading down the road. Where the van with my daughter would go I didn't have time to picture, because just then the man took a step towards me, those big muscled and tattooed arms beginning to reach for my daughter. Instinctively, I began to crouch and shift my weight and so ready myself for a karate kick to you-know-where. The man was bigger than I, but I had grown up in a tough neighborhood and had taken my share of judo and karate classes, and muscles don't mean everything when you're fighting for the life of your child.

Then, with surprising speed and grace, the man was right beside me, his grip tight on my wrist, forcing my hand to move higher up my daughter's slender neck.

"Hold her like this, man, so you cradle the head," the Hell's Angel nurse said, in a deep but surprisingly gentle voice. And then he let go of my wrist and with that same hand carefully pushed the hospital cloth aside so he could better see my daughter's face. "Oh, man," he said, "she's beautiful. Beautiful." And there was a kind of awe and certainty and quiet sadness in the way he said it that took all of the fear and apprehension out of me, so that when he held his arms out to me and said, "May I, man?" I gave my daughter to him as if he were the father and I the nurse.

He carried her into the Preparation Room and gently put her down on this kind of examining table, surprisingly full of low-tech things like scales and measuring tapes and color charts and vials of chemicals. The whole time he was bent over my daughter, weighing her and measuring her and gently, oh, so gently, swabbing the slime from her with these fluffy little gauze pads, he was carrying on this non-stop monolog-conversation (I couldn't tell whether he was talking to me and wanted an answer or to himself and needed none). "Oh, man, look at the color. The color. She's a nine, man. A nine. (This, I found out later was a way of measuring skin color in relation to anemia - 10 being the farthest away from anemia.) Look at that, man. Look at that. Ten beautiful fingers. Ten beautiful toes. It's all there, man. All there. The ears. The eyes. Oh, look at those eyes. Six pounds-eight, Man. Just the right size. Listen to the heart. Beating like a drum, man. Like a regular tom-tom. Center of the chart, man. Center of the chart."

And then he turned to me.

"You got a miracle baby here, man. Absolute miracle."

And then he held my daughter up to me, all pink and glowing in the humming light, and I saw what he meant. Everything was there, everything where it should be. Fingers. Toes. Eyes. Ears. All working. All the millions of cells doing what they should. The heart beating. The blood coursing. The brain and body working together to make life, human life, possible.

"Oh, man, you got a miracle here. You got a miracle baby," he said again, nodding his head as he handed her to me, positioning my daughter just so in my arms that my palm cradled the back of her head, as her eyes, her grey-brown eyes, flashed open and she saw me, her father, her lucky father, for the first time.

"You got a name for her, man?" the tattooed nurse said, a pen in his hand.

"Ariana," I said, unable to look away from my daughter.

"Beautiful, man. Beautiful. Ariana. Ariana. Two N's or one?

"One," I said. "It's Welsh. It means silver."

"Like her eyes, man. Like her eyes."

He wrote down more things on his chart and then he went over to a machine, a copy machine, I guess, and pressed the button and after a minute a copy came out which he brought over to me.

"For your records, man," he said.

My daughter had closed her silvery eyes and seemed to be asleep. Who wouldn't be weary after such an ordeal, I thought. A tough kid. She'll be a tough kid, having made it out of the womb like that, having survived the storm. And then I looked at the man, the Hell's Angel biker, the tattooed nurse.

"Don't take this wrong," I said, "but you're the last person on earth I'd ever expect to be an obstetric nurse."

The man looked at me a long moment and then he smiled and looked down at my daughter. When he spoke, it was in a soft voice, a faraway voice, and there was sadness in it. A deep sadness. What he was seeing, remembering, I could not imagine.

"I was in Viet Nam, man," he said, softly, slowly. "Medic." He looked up from my daughter to me. For the first time, I could see that he, too, had grey-brown eyes. "I've seen all the killing and maiming I ever want to." He paused. "When I came back, I knew this is where I wanted to be. Right here, man. Right here where life begins."

Neither of us said anything for a while. Maybe he was making that transition back from the killing fields where he had been to this shiny white hospital room devoted to life. I'd been spared the war but a lot of people I knew hadn't been. They'd come back scarred - body and soul. Maybe hearing all these first breaths of life would someday cancel out the memories of all those last ones.

The nurse, the tattooed obstetric nurse with big muscled arms, looked down again at my daughter, nestled safely in mine.

"Time to bring her to her mother, man," he said, smiling. "You want to carry her?"

"Forever," I said. "Forever."

Cathleen Calbert

Mermaid

When I was a girl, I was someone else: a mermaid swimming in the ivy.
Our house at Christmas became a charming inn, and I the innkeeper.
Then I was a witch, a witchy poet, a poet.

Then I thought I was truly a teacher, but now I pretend to teach. *This poem is really interesting,* I say, but the poem never is.

At home, I am my own maid, an editor hacking away at poems, and a wealthy retiree.

Am I really a writer? I don't know. I'm still the girl alone in the ivy, admiring my mermaid's tail.

Debby Thompson

Anne Frankenstein

When I open my journal, Anne emerges from her hiding place to hover at my shoulder. Does this happen to all female Jewish writers? I began to keep a journal at age 11 after reading The Diary. I named my journal Anna. "Dear Anna," I'd write, and then describe my pre-teen travails to Anne Frank in her voice.

"Terri Goodman whispered to Amy Bloom in the temple carpool that my hair looked greasy," I wrote.

"I still believe that people are good at heart," Anne replied.

It was hard to compete with the holocaust.

After I was bat mitzvahed at 13 I abandoned temple, along with much of Judaism. I've forgotten how to read Hebrew, and can't even get through the alphabet beyond aleph-bet-gimmel. But I still fast on Yom Kippur. And I still instinctively scan friends' homes for secret annexes.

I am now in my forties, and have been keeping a journal for thirty years. I don't call it Anna anymore; it's nameless. I write about the stabs of arthritis and of colicky colleagues, about my personal traumas and unutterable losses. But no monstrosities can compete with my progenitor. Anne, eternally thirteen, has left my shoulder and now burrows under my greasy scalp, the ultimate hiding place.

Approaching Home

Mark Saba

The Mindful House

I have been dreaming several times a month, for the past two or three years, about my grandmother's house. It's never the same dream, and many times my grandmother appears only obliquely—peeking around a corner, or sitting in her bedside chair reading her prayers—but these dreams always center on that house at the bottom of Margaret Street in the Mount Oliver section of Pittsburgh's South Hills.

My maternal grandmother died twenty-seven years ago. I was a freshman in college, and we buried her on January 14, 1977 at 10:00 AM, the coldest hour of the coldest day of the year. We heard on the news later, as water pipes froze in her empty house and stalled cars lined the city streets, that it had reached −17° F.

Brownsville Road is the busy thoroughfare that runs through Pittsburgh's closest south suburban hills, beginning in Mount Oliver, then passing through Carrick and Brentwood, where we lived, on the its way to Baldwin and Whitehall. It was, and still is, jam-packed with storefronts, gas stations, old brick homes with wide front porches, apartments, car dealers, cemeteries, bars, and churches. Riding along Brownsville road was like riding through a storybook, where every aspect of human life was brought to the fore. I observed it at least once a week, when we drove the three miles or so down Brownsville to get to Margaret Street, where Nana Kubiak lived.

As a child during the 1960's, standing or sitting in the back seat of my mother's aqua-colored Mercury Comet during those rides, I had a lot to take in. Each season offered its own cache of sensory perceptions. Winter rides meant I would hear the chorus of tire chains in snow, their steady rhythms as they approached, rang their tune, then faded. Cemeteries were barred. Gray clouds hung perennially over the city, smudges at the horizon where steeples and tall evergreens cut into them at the peaks of surrounding hills. Spring meant the car was warm as soon as you climbed into it, and everywhere— inside and out—I could smell the sun, its lingering dry dustiness surrounding me like a guardian angel. In summer our rides were more frequent; the car windows were open and warm air swirled into the sticky interior. Hills faded or disappeared behind thick foliage and haze: ink stains on the horizon. We stopped at the milk store, picked up a pizza for dinner, or passed through the great brick and stone archway to descend into the Polish cemetery, where my father lay. Once my mother ran a red light. Standing on the back seat and half-hanging out the partially opened window, I scowled at the policeman as he approached the car. My mother quietly burst into tears and apologized, explaining that she had never done that before, and that she had been preoccupied, a new widow with three children. He calmly wrote up the ticket, and as he passed by me on his way back to the flashing car I said, "Why did you make my mother cry?"

As I became older I would venture down to Brownsville Road alone, or with friends. We would buy ice cream cones, a new model at the Five and Ten, or a pack of baseball cards at the drug store. As we grew more daring we would ride our bikes for a couple of miles up and down Brownsville's hills, sometimes ending up at the Chevy and Buick car dealers so we could ogle over new models and test the patience of the men who worked there. And once, as a high school sophomore and member of the track team, I jogged down Brownsville Road to my grandmother's house, cut the grass, then jogged home.

Gertrude Radziukinas Kubiak, my grandmother, moved about slowly, but not aimlessly. She was her home's Commander-in-Chief. Born fourth in a line of fifteen children, 1902, and the first female, she eventually became a second mother to her copious siblings. They lived on the South Side of Pittsburgh in a wood-frame row house—same as every other Eastern European family—in three modest rooms. Though remaining conscientious in her duties assisting her Polish mother, Gertrude found time to have fun. She bowled, played baseball, and at eighteen, fell in love with Edmund Kubiak, whom she married in 1920.

Gertrude's first few pregnancies resulted in miscarriage, and her doctor, after careful diagnosis, announced that she was not fit to have children. Indeed, her own life may be in danger if she were to bring a child to term. Now Gertrude, unlike her drunken Lithuanian father and a number of her siblings, took her religion very seriously. She therefore ran from the doctor's office straight to the confessional to seek counsel on this outlandish ultimatum which would compromise her Catholic duty. Lucky for me, the priest advised her to ignore the doctor's warning, remain steadfast in prayer, and no harm would come to her in bearing children.

And he was right, for harm never came to my grandmother, though it did come to her children.

Nana Kubiak's entryway was painted a bright, unmistakable pink. White woodwork trimmed the walls and stairs; the carpet burned a deep red. My inclination, even as a child, was to hurry through it on the way to her blue kitchen with its promise of satisfying Polish fare, or to crash through the French doors that led from this hallway to her moss-colored living room.

A few things hung in that hallway: a small plastic basin filled with holy water, with its plastic virgin standing above; a faux gilded mirror set over a narrow, rounded ledge; and a portrait of some soldier in a dark frame, with a pair of swords crossed above him, and an inscription below. That man looked curiously like my mother. At some point I must have asked who it was, for I found out that it was indeed my mother's brother, who had died in World War Two, at Iwo Jima. As this was the mid-60's, I considered that war to be in league with dinosaurs and ice ages. My grandmother, as far as I remembered, had never spoken of this son of hers, whom they had called Junior.

In the moss-colored living room, where my grandfather often sat half-reclining on the embossed green couch, one leg tucked under him, watching Mutual of Omaha's Wild Kingdom or Lawrence Welk, a triptych of smaller picture frames rested top-center of their color console television. This triptych held the portraits of my mother and her two sisters, taken when they were in their early twenties. They each wore a velvet shoulder wrap and pearls. All were pretty. One was beautiful.

I knew that face. I had never needed to ask about it. It belonged to my Aunt Connie. She had been the one who came down the stairs with a brightly wrapped gift for me on my birthday, which I tore open to find a pair of alligator pajamas. How could I forget her! She had olive skin, bountiful black hair, and large, expressive black eyes. (My mother, by contrast, was fair.) I was secretly in love with her, in love with her memory. For I knew, all along, that she had also died.

Mindfulness, according to Bhante Gunaratana in his *A Guide to Buddhism,* is an "impartial watchfulness." He elucidates:

It does not take sides. It does not get hung up in what is perceived. It just perceives. Mindfulness does not get infatuated with the good mental states. It does not try to sidestep the bad mental states. There is no clinging to the pleasant, no fleeing from the unpleasant. Mindfulness treats all experiences equally, all thoughts equally, all feelings equally. Nothing is suppressed. Nothing is repressed. Mindfulness does not play favorites.

Could mindfulness be present in a home? If someone is always remembering everything that went on there, always aware that these past events are every bit as valid as those in the present—could that certain state of mindfulness eventually sink into the walls and easy chairs, the holy water basin and mirrors, the kitchen table, the echoless air?

When I walked into Nana Kubiak's house, I walked through a prism. Everything contained therein reflected something overwhelming, strong. It was not only a feeling I had, but rather an awareness of intense vigilance and comfort. And it was strange that my grandmother, who always wore a slightly worried look, could be prepared for anything: a Thanksgiving dinner, a card game, a side-splitting laugh, or a split-second peek into your soul. These emotions always came, however, behind that look of concern.

My childhood of the 1960's was full of concern, though not for reasons most people would imagine. The world outside my home and community was, to be sure, on the brink of turmoil, but everyone around me did their best to shield me from it. They gave me a warm home, a brightly lit school, and a network of family and friends who went about their business without minding much that which was outside their control. Pop culture came crashing through the television, or sounding from my hand-held turquoise transistor radio, but it always remained inside the television or radio. Rarely, if ever, did I hear anyone discussing at length the issues of the day. The parents of small children, teachers, priests, and grandparents all have better things to take care of.

One of those better things, it seems, was me.

A child's world, never challenged, becomes a solid perspective, however distorted, against which later years and experience are measured. The result, it seems, is that no other perception of reality, however grounded by adult consensus, can be as great.

Both my mother's parents and my parents married by their early twenties. Thus, I considered that the correct marrying age. My mother's friends and cousins married early also. Didn't everyone? My great-grandmother, I found out, had married at *fifteen*. Good Lord, there wasn't much time.

I saw photographs of many of these newlywed twenty-somethings from time to time—sitting on mantels in their silver lace frames, hanging in hallways, or held in place with small, white, gluey corners in the wedding album my mother kept in the Closet of Mysterious Things, just inside our front entryway. When I looked into that album of big black-and-whites, I saw the faces of my pretty mother and deceased father as newlywed adults, though today, as I remember, I would consider them one breath away from childhood. As I approached that "marrying age" of my childhood's perspective, it dawned on me that I was indeed still a child at twenty, and couldn't for the life of me conceive of marrying then. It was as if I'd been handed an extra decade or two to my life, an unexpected gift, for marriage seemed as far away to me then as Tokyo.

Still, the lives of my parents as newlyweds remained etched in my imagination for years, both during and after childhood. I thought of them as impecunious, hardworking, unaffected, and deeply in love. They were the offspring of European immigrants, Italian and Polish–Lithuanian, who found themselves in the American post-war world of new opportunity. My father worked his way through pharmacy school with the aid of a G.I. bill, and was the first in his family to marry outside of his Italian community. My mother, who played basketball, scrubbed her mother's floors, and longed for Tarzan movies on Saturday afternoons, took a streetcar half-way around the city to work in the drug store, far away from her Polish neighborhood, where she and my father met.

They had three children before he died, quite unexpectedly, of a brain tumor. The youngest, my brother, was eight months old at the time. That frozen newlywed love world of theirs has haunted me since. I was, for one thing, born of it.

If I stand at the bow of a sinking ship in a storm-wrecked sea with lightening intending to strike me down and the waters parting to swallow me up, I will remember at that moment that I was born of their love. This love-ghost resided in our house long after my father was gone, the very few images

I still had of him replaced by the legendary comments I often heard from relatives and my mother's friends. My sister, who was five when he died, remembers nearly falling from our borderless basement steps soon afterward, until she felt a cradling hand swoop up from the concrete floor to lift her to safety. There were the visual cues of his presence: a bottle of Old Spice still in the medicine cabinet, his first edition copy of *The Grapes of Wrath* lying in a box in the back of a closet, the crucifix that had hung above his coffin now in my bedroom. But the invisible cues were far more present: the looks I got from great aunts and uncles during their infrequent visits, whisperings when I went to another room, their voices lingering in my head. There was the absence of our '57 Bel-Air sedan, salmon and white, which my mother had traded in for the more modest Mercury Comet. I still saw the Bel-Air parked on the curve in the road in front of our house. At times I was certain I smelled a man's hair, or caught glimpses of a white shirt walking away from me, then turning around to wave goodbye.

Our house changed over the years. It lost its corners of cool, dark space which, though the house was small, existed in the quiet of Sunday mornings, summer afternoons, spring evenings. By the time I was ten my mother had remarried, and that monastic quality of our spare home was gradually supplanted by avocado kitchen appliances, shag rugs, a finished, faux-paneled basement, and heavy Spanish furniture. We grew into noisy teenagers. Radios blared; phones rang. And my grandmother still sat in her house on Margaret Street, alone now, crocheting soft blankets for her future great-grandchildren's cribs.

Now that I could drive, I was elected to take her on errands occasionally, as well as clean her windows, wash her kitchen walls, and plant her tomato plants. I also, in my new adolescence, began to see things in her house differently. I opened cabinets and peered inside; checked the contents of kitchen drawers; inspected each of the forty or so sets of salt and pepper shakers she collected and displayed in a nook full of narrow shelves.

One of my best finds was her collection of 78 rpm records, those oddly-sized black discs, thick and heavy, with dark blue or orange labels in deco sans-serif type. I found The Andrew Sisters, Gershwin, Benny Goodman, and Louis Armstrong, among others. I was even able to coax her old console stereo back into use to hear them play. Marveling at the musical taste of my grandparents (I loved every one of these records) I became more interested in the aesthetic of that time period. As someone who heard anything from The Bee Gees to Bachman Turner Overdrive on the radio, I wondered what kind of lives my grandparents and others had had as youths. What kind of society had produced the silky vocals of Ella Fitzgerald and the haunting beauty of Greta Garbo? What about Aaron Copland, John Steinbeck? Each of these artists seemed to have arrived at a level of dignified and absolute beauty that I hadn't been able to detect in any era since. Was my grandmother somehow rooted in that aesthetic sense? I bought my own, 33 rpm versions of Louis

Armstrong and The Andrew Sisters, and lost myself in that distant, grayscale world as my friends blasted their Aerosmith and Kiss.

The last thing she said to me was *Don't miss mass before going on a trip.* I was headed for Florida and New Orleans, where the University of Pittsburgh was slated to play in the Cotton Bowl. Not a fanatic sports fan by any means, my sole intent for making this trip was to see palm trees. My grandmother sat at my aunt's kitchen table (as Eastern Europeans often do), looking, as usual, a bit worried. I had no reply. I was to meet my small gang of college buddies very early the next morning. No time for mass.

Crossing over the Florida border after twenty-some hours in a crowded car, I saw two short, struggling palms planted on either side of the welcome sign. Six hours later, in West Palm Beach, I saw plenty of the real McCoy. We swam in our friend's parents' condominium pool, sat in a dry heat sauna, drank beer, swam some more. In New Orleans we passed out on the palmetto bug-infested floor of a fraternity house after having celebrated not only the New Year, but Pitt's victory as well. Finally, we drove home in a southern ice storm, the likes of which I had never seen, with cars spinning like magnets, each encased in a thin, clear shell, everywhere we looked.

Having arrived safely home, my mother confessed to having kept some information from me: Nana Kubiak had had a stroke a few days into my trip. She now lay in intensive care, comatose.

I had bought her a set of salt and pepper shakers in Louisiana: small brown glass barrels with metal lids. She let go after nine days, just as I was embarking on a new semester at Pitt.

I went through the grieving process, if I did at all, in a kind of trance. My freshman year at the university had offered me freedom and a new strength of character; my head was still reeling from it. And my trip to the American south had thrilled my soul, awakening a new wanderlust in me that would find further expression in the years to come. I was simply not in the mood for a funeral.

Weeks later I found myself sitting in my General Writing class reading our next assignment: to describe something using three different points of view.

I chose my grandmother's house. My first description was a tidy little paragraph of the sort that realtors use to market their product: two stories with walk-up attic, French doors, an addition out the back, two full baths, etc. It was cold and humorless, as intended. In my second description I took a more literary approach, beginning with the yard and its one great evergreen, the green and white cloth awnings hanging around the wide porch, the yellow brick, the quiet end of an inclined street. All the details I chose, however, pointed to stillness, a snapshot, a lifeless shell hinting of death.

My third description escapes me just now, but I imagine it was what I considered to be the most "accurate" of the three, describing one of the Sunday dinners we had there, as well as its attending characters: my quiet great Uncle

Tony who lived in the attic, Aunt Florence who often spontaneously broke out into song, my grandfather trying to get me to use his snuff as one of his many cures for my asthma, or my sister dropping our ration of priceless *czarnina*, a Polish soup made of duck's blood, onto the kitchen floor.

Or might I have described instead the house my mother grew up in: her brothers getting up in the middle of the night to shovel coal into the furnace, the mini beauty pageants the three lovely daughters put on for their uncles once a year (my Aunt Connie always won), the hush that fell over the house as my great-grandfather listened to wartime radio broadcasts for news about Poland, or the caskets laid out in the living room containing a set of twins only days old.

I might have chosen also to describe Nana Kubiak as she sat in her overheated house crocheting, the furnace ticking after it stopped blowing, wind picking up outside. She might have been quite content sitting there figuring out a new pattern, while the ghosts of her children tumbled over one another in play, her husband called from the bedroom, fast friends gathered at her kitchen table for a night of Thirty-One, or her mother peeked around a corner to spy her with the eyes of a stranger in the grips of Alzheimer's.

Thomas Merton wrote, "If there were no humility in the world, everybody would long ago have committed suicide," for "humility alone can destroy the self-centeredness that makes joy impossible." This Christian humility may be linked to the Buddhist notion of mindfulness, or "impartial watchfulness." If you are humble yet mindful, as I believe my grandmother was, you do not dwell on your misfortunes, yet neither do you forget them. You simply go on, letting those ghosts have the run of the house, as you labor to stitch together something new, something artful and loving. And in that pattern you choose, and the colors represented, you will have included everything you are mindful of.

So my grandmother's hands work frantically, as they always have, against time, weaving blankets, afghans, scarves, hats, and little bells to hang on her French doors at Christmastime—things to protect, warm, and enliven us; things to cushion us against misfortune and pain, making it a little easier for us to embrace whatever life may dish up in a future she cannot predict, but loves just the same.

52

Sheryl L. Nelms

Outhouse Blues

so much of my early
life was spent
suspended

above that black
and gargoyled
pit

hanging there
in the cold ammonia draft

remembering the horror
stories of a cousin
who disappeared
forever

when he was
grabbed
from

below

Maureen Tolman Flannery

Fishing for Father

Ruby Devine

We who thought we knew him well
would have said of him,
despite his kindness and his passion
for the charms of women,
that he was hamstrung by
an inability to love just one.

We had heard the laundry list of old conquests—
high school sweethearts, college betrotheds,
war receptive foreigners from vast continents
he navigated and touched down upon.

Never of mention of this name
a name I knew vaguely
from remote and indistinct regions
of childhood recollection,
a name that conjures exotic jewels and sanctity,
one that might belong to an Indian saint
or a San Francisco fan dancer.

He never spoke of her to his daughters.
Was hers the name too sacred to say,
water too profound to be waded into,
ground too hallowed to tread.

Was her name the sequestered treasure
in the lock-box of his memory
to be taken out in reverie or prayer
and reexamined as an heirloom or a priceless artifact.
Was hers the life-love
the withholding of which
unhinged and crazed my mother?

Comparing Memories with the Half-Sister

There was breach in his being, a fissure
between the secrets and a man unlikely to have them.

Two sisters and their half-sister, formerly unknown,
might miter the misfit edges,

join the separated corners of a life already over,
pull fallibility into the frame of his goodness.

Their discordant recollections could, even now,
piece together

the light-hearted life of everyone's party
with the sullen spouse who'd walk out on his wife's questions

the dutiful husband
with the passionate lover of some other life

the dance-with-me dad
with the unacknowledged giver of mysterious gifts

the respected family man
with the clandestine care-taker of someone else's family

the charmer
with the man disarmed by what might come to pass

the fisherman
with one unable to clean his own catch

the rancher
with the man who brought provisions to the hired man's shed

the admired community leader
with the meeter of strangers in dark places

the church elder
with the self-blaming, self-proclaimed sinner.

Invite them all to the table,
the altar where we are all related.

The Golden Age of Country

A boxed set of old country hits
and my lips are syncing every melancholy lyric
of rejection, loss, just-missed happiness—
songs about being a rounder, a rover,
a guitar-toting jerk, or being done wrong,
being hurt, being a fool or an all-around loser,
about cheatin' and leavin' or stayin' and deceivin'.
honky-tonkin' as a life-style, a tear-dryin' night,
as a way to forget or get back in the game—

And I am rattling out to the badland with dad
in that old pickup
or on the way up to the cabin in late spring,
my father, the cowboy driver,
making new roads around gullies of run-off
or straddling deep ruts with two wheels in the center
and two on the outside in new greening grass,
his transistor radio between us on the seat,
the two of us jostling along singing aloud
to every song on the all-country station,
both obliviously off key and not caring a wit—
I am safe and happy and completely unaware
of how dad, in his handsome prime,
might be finding himself in the lyrics of these
done-wrong and been done-wrong
heartache songs.

Letter

A letter arrived.
clues, guesses, suspicions, innuendo,
imparted news--
not news,
old truths
and perhapses and what ifs
things we should have known
and things we cannot know.

And I don't know what to do with it,
where to go with my new half-knowing.
Participants, long dead, don't confirm or deny.
They squirm at first, then encourage us to know them
in their blessed imperfections,
kick up spirit dust in the air they loved into,
shove us toward what matters
in the midst of matter they cannot manipulate.

This letter strips me naked.
It rips my story down the middle,
spatters it with lamb's blood and copper-colored mud,
then takes it from the basket into afternoon light
scrubs it clean again and mends it,
squeezes my story through an old hand-cranked wringer
and smoothes it moist and wrinkle-free to bleach in the sun
on a pile of firewood behind the cabin.
It dangles in front of me my sun-dried story,
stiff and smelling of lye soap and alfalfa
and expects me to put it on again.

Test Results

Eighty-five percent probability of sibling kinship

85% accurate accusation that my father
was loving another woman when I was one year old

a cold hard DNA explanation
for my mother's possessive hold on her own girls
why she became ever more demanding
and less content as he met each new demand

15% chance her reactions were irrational

low odds his heart was ever hers after that
high likelihood she always felt unloved
had reasons for not trusting
for thrusting herself into the arms of her church

genetic explanation for her chronic displeasure
with a seemingly easy life
why she didn't encourage me to be a ranch girl
never wanted him to go fishing

85 degrees of silent rage that seethed inside my mother's psyche
and made her seem the crazy one

high odds that the lives of all involved were complicated
by the possibility of this probability

85 creases in the portrait he wanted saved
innumerable reasons for holding his secrets
one answer to the question he took to the grave

0% probability my childhood can actually have been
what I believed it to be

Sarah L. Webb

Lineature

Theory of Relatives

Arms spread out like queens on a cross, we shut our
eyes and spun until spacetime shifted,

calling, "Siisstaahh!" and hoping that our
orbits would collide. If we spun faster

our gravity for each other would increase. Our
rotations suddenly halted when spacetime ripped,

dropping us in the front yard, dizzy, as our
scapes slowly reverted to stasis. I studied our relative

positions in the grass to determine if our
axis had precessed. It seemed that our relative

motion could break time. Yet here we are.

Lucy Anna and Me

They don't understand what we be
saying, sha. They could

never get down
with how we suck them heads

pinch tails and, guh,
how we zydeco.

We say: Please excuse our French
quartered like quadroons passing

through cypress tress strung up
with Spanish moss and black bodies swinging

out. From the front porch we see the streets
flooding. They aint seen rain

till they packed sandbags in front they doors,
had main thoroughfares turn into shallow

tributaries of the Mighty Mississippi,
cars moving at the speed of barges

along the German Coast. Cash crops
King Cotton and cane sugar sweetened life

for them too. They can't take the cayenne
heat boiling in this pot of boudin, baby.

We gone give them the Boot
cause they aint from round here

Le Nom

Diaspora articulates, or bends together, both roots and routes . . .
Emmanuel Akyeampong , "Defining Diaspora"

My grandfather had a red baseball cap with his name monographed Efern. A 1910 census spells it Ephraim, possibly based on the biblical character found in the book of Genesis, the book of origins. But our history is largely speculation, no canonized genealogy. There is no birth certificate from 1908, the year we believe my grandfather was born in Saint Martinville, Louisiana. On the census I read and reread the names of family living in his boyhood home, trying out different pronunciations: Louis 29, Alosia 25, Henry 12, Silvanie 10, Rena 9, Louis 6, Arsene 4, Ephraim 2. Spellings changed every ten years, illegitimate names of the illiterate, derivatives of the actual sign, oral traditions translated through transcription. How to spell? How to articulate?

I imagine the Census Collector riding up to the shack in a horse drawn carriage. Most of the family is already outside, Louis and Arsene playing in the mud, a neighbor or two sitting on the front porch chatting with my great grandmother in creole who's holding my grandfather on her hip. The Census Collector trudges toward them through muddy government obligation, calling out for the head of the household. My great grandfather is probably away working. My great grandmother is suspicious and calls for Silvanie, the oldest daughter, to tell her what this white man is talking about.

The Census Collector wants to hurry this process along. He's uncomfortable around all the filth and ramshackle and he still has six more households to visit before he can return to his brick home and to his family and bathe. "Can you tell me the names of everyone living in this house, their ages, and their relationship to the head of household?" He writes down what he hears, often initiating a back and forth pronunciation register:

"Sylvannia."

"Sylvania?"

"Silvania."

"Sylvannie?"

until embarrassment or frustration makes him amalgamate all of the pronunciations he's heard with his possibly French influenced palate (or palette, which is essentially the same when it comes to language). He thanks them and leaves with a headache from the concentration it took to comprehend and endure that tedious interview. But I could be wrong.

Ledet is my grandfather's surname, the name we use to define ourselves. It's the Americanized version of the French word Le Dé, a nickname for a gambler, meaning the dice. Now, in our family at least, we've even

Americanized the pronunciation with an audible t. We always call our reunions "Ledet Family reunions" regardless of how many of us actually bear that name. When a relative is especially soulful in dance or song, we tell them, "You got that Ledet blood in you." But where does this blood really come from? Our love for music and dance is appreciated as a remnant of some African origin, but it's quite possible that the actual Ledet bloodline is not originally African.

Of course Ledet includes my grandmother, whom the family sometimes calls Lorena Williams to acknowledge her maiden name. But the offspring of my grandparents invariably take the name of the Patriarch. He's our origin, and from there we are dispersed, taking on new identities that never completely elide the original.

62

de'fine line

de'fine line
drooping line dripping with polka-dotted panties, paisley dress, and clothespins
outline sketch of this still life
pulling thread through till it's tight, lining the garment with linen, securing the seam
roads stitching places into a narrative quilt
cartography of lineage
frown lines engraved on a dark young face, forehead furrowed in aching, oppressive thought
intersecting lines from Australia
waiting in line for a connection to
Louis Armstrong International Airport in New Orleans
by definition, this should have no end
stopped on the bridge at night
clouds over industrial land resemble paintings of apocalyptic explosions
what's the first line of defense
no more running unless home
no more running unless through fields of dandelion seeds
country roads trace a hitchhiker's journey
longitudinal legs
unlike an arrow; like a bow
no thickness
drawn with a brown crayon
slightly parallel
damp meridian marks on a face, jagged contours as a river flowing south
coursing a global head
equating experiences
locating latitude
i struggle to connect even when the line is dotted with reflectors
spotted
with spotted cows, pine trees, and mist
according to the legend
marks on a map

Rails and Ties

Roads and train tracks delineated part of my history down near the Gulf Coast. I was first made aware of this during our family reunion in July 2009 when we rented a charter bus to take us from Lafayette, Louisiana, to Memphis, Tennessee. My mother had me act as tour guide, announcing to the family as we passed through Hammond, Louisiana, that Grandpa helped build these roads. The road my grandfather helped build in Hammond is presently known as Interstate 12, an intrastate highway, that stretches east and west a mere eighty-five miles within the state of Louisiana between Baton Rouge and Slidell, passing along the northern shore of Lake Pontchartrain. For five years I drove on I-12 from Baton Rouge to Hammond, where it intersects with Interstate 55. From there I'd head north on I-55, then east on Highway 25 until I reached my destination at Mississippi State University in Starkville. I think, my grandfather literally paved the way.

Local Weather

These are not electric cities,
not even when it rains.

Here, the ground may be edgy,
but the atmosphere is languid,

silent and cool, though incandescent.
Here is manufactured luminosity,

a commodity necessarily sold
with a higher degree

of blindness, a shimmering, fulsome
mist with a quarter mile of visibility or less.

Yards and Porches

The original address of my grandparents' house was 316 Argon Street in Lafayette, Louisiana. When they moved in, the house probably cost less than $10,000, but there's no telling what they paid in interest. My mom was in high school or college by the time they got a kitchen sink and she said they heated their bath water on the stove. Since then, the address has changed to 1710 Twelfth Street, and several updates have been made to the house. When my aunt, who still resides there, bought a clothes dryer, I remembered the clothesline that had stretched the width of the yard for years. We played in the backyard all the time in those days and our games were either "in front of the clothesline" or "on the other side of the clothesline" depending on how much yard we required for a particular game. Adding to the element of adventure in our games was the challenge of not accidentally pulling down the already sagging clothesline.

We spent many summers playing, eating, talking, and dancing on the front porch. In fact, the kids were often locked out and ordered to play and eat outside so we wouldn't dirty up the house. Cold cups (like a popsicle in a cup, about 200% sweeter) were the worst and the best. We'd ask the grown ups for change, about fifty cents I believe, and we'd all go around the corner to some lady's house who sold cold cups and candy from her window. Back at the house, we'd sit on the steps and the syrupy juice would drip and get sticky around our mouths, on our fingers, and down our legs.

Naturally, the porch was always the outdoor stage where we performed the dances we'd made up and practiced in the backyard. The porch was usually "base" for the various forms of tag we used to play. We even invented a game once, called "drive by" where we stood on the sidewalk and every time a car passed by we ran toward the house yelling "drive by!" and took cover on the porch.

From aia.org 2009

Architects
14% licensed female architects
1% licensed African-American architects
4% licensed Asian architects
3% licensed Hispanic architects

Associates
33% of Associate AIA members are women
3% of Associate AIA members identify as African-American
8% of Associate AIA members identify as Asian
8% of Associate AIA members identify as Hispanic

At Mississippi State, undergraduate architecture students took Architecture History 1 in our second year, though several students repeated the course and were third years. Without a doubt, the class kicked people's butts. It was notoriously difficult and half the class would usually fail the first test. I got to class early on the day we were to receive our first grades and sat in the first row of the auditorium like always. Professor McCann approached me smiling, "You got the only A in the class, you brain." I got a 97 and the next highest grade was nine points below mine. It felt good to dominate the white man's realm for a moment. I mean that. Up until then, only a handful of white guys had been considered "the brains." I remember one of them suggesting to me, "You could like bomb on the next test and still have a good grade." But he wasn't fooling anybody. People flocked to me in preparation for the next exam. How did I do it? Could I join their study group? I couldn't really help them though. I attribute my success in that class largely to my insatiable desire to know the material.

Architecture 1 was quite multicultural and I think that's why I took to it. Professor McCann was one of my favorite teachers, though I'd heard a couple of those white guys complaining about her "feminism." I thought – sure, complain if you consider including women in the telling of history to be radically feminist instead merely logical. These guys were obviously offended that Professor McCann would acknowledge that some societies privileged the feminine and expressed that in their architecture. As our study moved along chronologically, though, the male dominated Western world was re-centered and I eventually lost my appetite for studying architecture history.

Major Changes

I cried when I changed my major from architecture to English. Two and a half years into my undergraduate career, about a decade of commitment, a decade of constructing my identity around my future career as an architect, someone who could design the buildings that fascinated her, and then nothing. No direction, no purpose, no goal other than to finish college.

I played my favorite Nina Simone song on repeat: I see my light come shining from the west down to the east. Any day now, any day now, I shall be released. I filled my mom's bathtub with hot water and sulked in it until she came home from work and found me, my fingers pruning, my forehead perspiring from all the steam. I broke down when I told her "I'm not going to be in architecture any more." She, more than anyone, understood the power behind the dream that appeared to be in pieces.

Sonnet Across 41st Street

Reading on the front steps, deliberately
Framed in sun, anthologized, paper thin
Art for the sake of informality

Across 41st
When you come around the block, brothers clown a lot
The guys, their parked stereos

Blues, gradient, roof lines
We're all reciting, I know, those verses
This text I'm beating with my fingers

I gave her my pipe dream of how I'd write
A script and make it to the bright screen
In this climate, screens are rare

Rest this book on bent knees so
I can keep my head up.

Literature

I write what my grandfather built. Passages. He paved a way for me to go places he never could. So I go. To Starkville, San Francisco, Oakland, educating myself in reading and writing. Word by word traversing the land and the page with inter-marginal lines. Spelling my own name.

Road: A long, winding, narrow, clearing away of wildness that gives an oblique and transitory awareness of the world; a place of connectivity; an avenue; a language. I arrived at this place, the history of this place without words. My hope is to leave with miles and miles of language between us.

Kerry Trautman

Approximate Biography

One Way to be Raised

I was raised
with day-long simmered soup
and strawberry patches
that became jam in July.

I was raised
with a crabapple treehouse
that grew bigger, shakier,
eventually was just for boys.

I was raised
with a gravel driveway
mudpuddles for play
and stray cats porch to porch.

I was raised
with a pink-bead rosary in my nightstand
and purple and gold irises in spring.

I was raised
with grandma's robust knitted sweaters
and my first read novel about
a mouse far away from home.

I was raised
with jigsaw puzzles for weeks
with mountain peaks and blazing maples.

I was raised
with Cheers before bed
and Carson after.

I was raised
with Barbies on a blanket outside
and haphazard plays with backdrops of
billowing clothesline sheets.

I was raised
with the entire outside in sunlit hours
shut back in each dusk.

Gone Camping

Mom sneaked beers into the campground—
just two—for after dark, for sipping
with s'mores, while we sipped orange soda.
Mom lounged, having left Dad behind
with the laundry piles, cats and unpaid bills,
content to stare at the fire, feed it lopped logs,
feed us canned hash and powdered donuts.
We kids played poker, wagered pretzel sticks,
through vast, starry hours without clocks,
wakened by eventual sun and lure of the beach.

We knew there was planning—lists on yellow
legal pads, the geometry of cramming blankets,
folded aluminum chairs, cots, cooking pots,
sweaters for fire-time, and bundled branches
in the boxy van—but it wasn't up to us.
Now, camping isn't hopping, shoeless, in the van.
Now the planning, the lists of atypical foods,
the goading of my children who fear dark, insects,
the tent to pitch and dismantle, the cleaning and
stowing of gear after—is chaos in my tidy life.

When I camp now, it is for my mom.
To repay her for her years of laundering sandy
sleeping bags, pillows dusted in blown ash—
as if I owe her for our escapes and her own.
As if she had needed us there to witness her
perched on her unfolded chair, watching waves
tumble themselves two-by-two ashore,
but never wading herself in, never patting-firm
the sands of our castles, dredging our moats,
never calling "Polo" to our "Marcos."

One August, the day my neighborhood was
awakened at two a.m. by torrents of rain,
by basements five-feet full with murky water,
furnaces gurgling their drowning deaths,
boxes of outgrown shoes and Christmas
tinsel sunk like pirates' doubloons, the day
the Blanchard River engulfed our town and others
upstream and down, the day thousands lost
their sweaters and cats, cars and mattresses,

I was supposed to have gone camping.

My van dutifully crammed, Mom, on high ground,
furious when I called, said my roads were the river.
Helicopters surveyed. Boat wakes sloshed Main St.
storefronts. Families fled soup homes to shelters,
camped on flat cots, sobbed on CNN, waited days to
slog home, to shovel their walls bare, to drag moldy
rubble to piles, curbsides mounded with blackened
chairs, pianos and dolls, garbage trucks constantly
rumbling. Yet I was only me, disappointing her
in her city, somewhere beyond all of my water.

Renny Murphy Golden

Murphy's Music

After he had a stroke in the late 1940s, my grandfather, Denis (Dinny) Murphy, retired from the union he'd founded. He was a mess. The stroke caused him to lurch to one side when he walked, and if that weren't odd enough, he occasionally would take from his eye socket the glass eye he'd lost as a result of influenza.

"Put it back in Pa, please put it back!" my cousins and I squealed when he held the eyeball out to us.

I don't know what he felt about his ruined body. He no longer called the Ceili set dances, nor whirled into a hornpipe or jig. Before, Pa was thick waisted, pot-bellied, but light on his feet, his steps quick and he could kick high. After the stroke, he dragged one leg behind him and he wove down Dante Street like a drunken sailor. His step dancing days were over.

Dinny began Local #399 (boiler-men) in Chicago with Richard Wren in the 1930s. Wren, not Dinny, was the brains of the outfit. Wren was related to the knighted Irishman Sir Thomas Wren. He set up contracts, learned labor law, and met with city officials. Dinny supplied the brawn---Irish immigrants willing to feed the furnaces of hotels, schools, and hospitals. Pa often gave the boys room and board until they had paychecks. They all owed him. It made him important.

It was Dinny Murphy, not Wren, who was the workingman's comrade. I know this because I know the story of the Republic Steel strike in 1937. I have imagined my grandfather's role in that strike based on my mother's story and my growing up near the mills. In the spring of 1937 my grandfather boarded a Stony Island trolley car headed for South Chicago. As a labor organizer he planned to attend the Republic Steel Memorial Day picnic in order to show solidarity, he said, with "the poor devils" who been on strike for months. The steelworkers were fighting Tom Girdler of Republic Steel who refused to accept the union even though, nationally, steelworkers had successfully joined the AFL-CIO. Girdler, according to Dinny, was a "steel-hearted bastard" who defied both John L Lewis and the Wagner Act. Worse than that, in my grandfather's eyes, Girdler was a coward because he had the Chicago police on his side against unarmed workers.

Dinny transferred to a bus at 87th street and sat by the window. He changed buses once, and then walked down 101st Street past the two-flat boarding houses that stood shoulder to shoulder like exhausted workers. He expected his boys to meet him at the picnic grounds in the field next to Republic Steel. Families had spread blankets and wicker baskets on the grass; police paddy wagons were parked along the edge of the field. Spirits were as high as the kites young boys were flying. Murphy glanced up at a turquoise sky which was dotted with diamond-shaped flyers wagging their tails of old socks. The kids' jubilance bolstered their discouraged parents' spirits. After the long days of winter and the months without a salary, the picnic was renewing. Some workers had been ready to give up because they couldn't depend on relatives to feed their families much longer. The wives brought baskets of kielbasa, pigs' feet, and pasta--- a splurge in the midst of their ordeal. It was the best act of jubilance and resistance the strike leaders could manage.

Dinny found his buddies from Local #399 and took the pint of Harp they offered. They shook their heads, worried. "My God, Dinny, they have half the force out and this is a solidarity picnic!" One of the strike leaders shook hands with Dinny. They knew him because he was one of the organizers for the Micks' (Irish) Local. But that day Dinny Murphy was not clannish. America's worker underdogs were his comrades: Polish organizers, Jewish communists, Italians who tended the blast furnaces. Most were immigrants whose families crowded into small wood framed houses in South Chicago. The single ones lived in boarding houses on the Southeast side, walked to Lake Michigan beaches on Sundays in the summer. They had little else.

Dinny knew about the Molly Maguires, Irish workers in the late 1800s who blew up bridges to protest starvation wages. He knew the Molly Maguire leaders were shot or hung. But that was years ago and no worker had been shot in Chicago since the Haymarket protest in the late 1800s. Dinny expected harassment, nothing more. He was familiar with the odds: unarmed workers against the police and the bosses. This time, it was disquieting to know that the men with guns were Irish.

As Dinny sipped his pint, he watched the blue line of policemen move in a circle around the gathering. All was peaceful, so most were not alarmed. The union leaders didn't think the police would harm women and children. Still the workers moved toward the periphery as a wall between themselves and the picnickers.

Strike leaders moved toward the plant and much of the crowd processed behind. Some sang, boys ran up the line poking each other. Their mothers called them back to no avail. When the procession approached the police line surrounding the plant entrance they held up.

Without warning, the cops charged the crowd, goaded by an officer named Prendergast. Mothers pulled the children from the surge, running from cops swinging batons and Billy clubs. Baskets of chicken were spilled; potato salad splattered the strikers' boots; children cried, and women screamed. Then the shots rang out.

A bullet hit Leon Franchesco's faded work shirt, a stain opening like a rose. Sam Popovitch couldn't run fast enough. When a Billy club caught him, he fell holding his smashed skull, the dying eyes astonished. An accordion winced where workers pushed Dolan from a line of shots.

76

Steelworkers pulled the fallen Sam Causey into someone's car but cops dragged him bleeding back onto the street. Otis Jones and nine others would not see the strike end. They died on a picnic field.

Dinny came home to my grandmother ashen, ruffled, his fingers still knotted in fists when he spoke.

"My God, Missus," Dinny told my grandmother, his disbelief still shocking him, "they shot the boys in the back."

"Who gave the orders, Dinny?"

"A dirty dog named Prendergast carried them out. But the bastard who had the lads killed was Captain Mooney. There's your respectable Irishman, Annie."

The next day, the *Chicago Tribune*--- owned by Colonel Robert McCormick--- reported that the workers had provoked the police.

* * * * *

In the late 1940s my grandparents spent their summers at my Aunt Helen's cottage on a lake in northern Wisconsin. All the Murphys and their families gathered there, too. We children loved the sentinels of white birch that lined the calla Lilly-covered swamp-side of Lake Eau Claire. We loved the smell of the woods on rainy days and the long rose twilights fingering through evergreens in August. Mostly we loved my grandmother's lamb, Timmy.

"Damndest thing I've ever seen," said Dinny whom we called Pa. "Missus still thinks she's in Mullingar where they raised sheep. What the hell is she going to do with Timmy when he gets big? Off to the butcher!"

"No, Pa, don't say that!" we screamed.

My grandmother, who ruled, continued to feed Timmy with a baby bottle. She rolled her eyes at Dinny's complaints as if having a lamb as a pet was not a bit unusual.

"It's you, Murphy, who has never left the old country," she said dismissively.

When Timmy trotted toward the woods, my grandmother's collie ran circles around the nervous Timmy, herding him back to her. We clapped.

Dinny said, "It's a goddamn circus!"

Once my Aunt Helen, hoping to find Dinny a friend to keep him company, invited an old Irishman from Chicago's Southside for a visit. Aunt Helen told me the story about what happened that day twenty-five years later. Because labor history was lost, she didn't know its social meaning. To her it was just an example of her father's "fighting Irish spirit." This is the story.

"There's another Chicago Irishman from across the lake that I'm asking for breakfast tomorrow, Pa. I thought you'd like to meet him," my Aunt said.

Dinny nodded absently.

The next morning when my Aunt saw the old man leaning on his cane as he walked toward their yard, she called to Dinny who was in the back of the house. Apparently she hadn't mentioned the gentleman's name until then.

"Pa, he's here now, Captain Mooney is here."

With that my grandfather pulled himself through the house, knocking down chairs, the rag doll leg stumping crookedly. He threw open the door, eyes blazing.

"Pa, my God, what's wrong?"

He bent down and picked up a large stick. He hobbled out to the road, drew a line in the sand and looked Mooney straight in the eye, then raised the stick to emphasize every word.

"Don't ye set yer murderous foot over that line, ye bastard, or I'll kill ye on the spot, the way you killed the workers of Republic Steel."

Mooney, the enforcer of lines that dare not be crossed, turned and left. Captain Mooney did not look back at the old man still waving a stick, daring him to cross the line.

Dinny's youngest daughter, Helen, had been away at school at the time of the Republic Steel strike and she had no memory of its significance. When she finished the story, I was crying.

"He still remembered," I said quietly.

"Remembered what?" my aunt asked.

"Whose side he was on," I said.

It was the last line my grandfather would draw. He died of another stroke later that year.

* * * * *

My grandfather was the first music I heard. Not just that he sang Irish rebel songs but he was a kind of music to me. Clomping down the street, like a lopsided, scarred old donkey, his presence sang to me. I remember our "concerts" listening to the great tenor, John McCormick.

I was five years old, sitting next to Pa on the couch with crocheted white lace doilies that "protect" the armrests. "Leave us alone, Missus," Pa said to my grandmother. Smiling to find us there, she tiptoed away as if the moment were holy. Shadows pool in the parlor where we listened to John McCormick's trebling tenor sing "Macushla." The parlor was brushed with streetlight gold and outside, the last ribbons of plum clouds opened night's door. I still can hear my aunts and uncles laughing in the kitchen--- the music of my childhood like a far off circus, all clowns and acrobats flung through the air, circus animals that are never sad. Yet I did not want to be in the kitchen. Pa rewound the Victrola again, placed the arm carefully, and McCormick's voice filled the spaces of ocean, Dingle cliffs, the brocade fields of Kerry. Pa would sing with McCormick, barely reaching the high notes: "Mavourneen, mavourneen the grey dawn is breaking, the grey dawn is breaking Kathleen Mavourneen. It may be for years or it may be forever."

Then tears would trickle down his chin. Suddenly he'd wipe his eyes and, as if the bearers of so much sorrow should pay, he'd sing a rebel song, slapping his knee with his fist. If I knew the chorus I'd sing along, very loudly: "Come all ye young rebels and list while I sing, how the love of one's country is a terrible thing, it banishes fear like the touch of a flame, and that's why I'm part of the patriot's game."

His memories and the songs follow him unshakable as his childhood sheep dog. He carries his mother's songs, too, the way I carry his, as a kind of defiance. His mother was born in the shadow of Black '47 (1847) when the potato crop failed a third time and Ireland starved. Half of her people died or left in those years. He carries her stories of village babies too weak to bawl, mothers mad with typhoid begging in the roads, priests who cut the sod by day, rode the Killarney circuit at night to bury the dead and offer consolation to those who bore the abyss, wild eyed with grief.

Pa's memory is like the donkey at his mother's farm, all stubborn, bent from the creels of bog carried over the soaked land again and again, his weather beaten flanks, scarred. He carries it all: resist every blow, plod on, walk the heathered fields, the wild coast of Ballinskelligs. Pa has fled the sod-laden baskets, the master's stick, and Killarney too, with her gulls and swallows sweeping Dingle. He cannot say any of this. McCormick sings it for him. I don't know all of this at five but I sense in Pa a love of one's land and people that is, as Yeats said, "deep in the heart's core."

* * * * *

Dinny Murphy's stroke had left him fit enough to drag his partially paralyzed leg up and down basement stairs to fix boilers and shovel coal for the widowed Mrs. Finnegan and the Brannigan family. He was a boiler man again. Back to where he started when he came to this country. An Irish peasant with a strong back, a sense of humor and fierce loyalty.

Even now, I can see Pa limping down Dante Avenue under a canopy of maple trees. His tonsure of white and peach red hair is caught by morning sunlight as he lumbers toward Mrs. Finnegan's three-flat. There are coal stains on his denim overalls and he is turning to tell the carrot-top skipping beside him, "We could sing, lassie, just to see if you remember the songs."

We descend into Mrs. Finnegan's basement and Pa is humming. The coal is hip high piled into a black mound that walls off a section of the basement. Still humming he opens the flame whooshing furnace door, then swings in a shovel-full.

"Now," he says, "sing the chorus with me because it's clear you don't remember the verses."

I pick up coal pieces, sooting my polo shirt, throw them into the open mouth, and in my best rhythm to match his shoveling and singing, I sing along, "Ah come out ye Black and Tans, come out and fight me like a man..."

Then I fake the next two lines I forgot and shout the last lines with him "and how the IRA made ye run like hell away..."

"Better," he says. "Now Roddy McCorley" which I don't know at all.

The tame, silly songs like "Paddy McGinty's Goat," however, were why my first grade teacher called my mother.

"Mrs. Golden, I just wondered where she learned the song," Sister Margaret said on the phone.

"What was the song, Sister?" my mother asked, puzzled.

"It was some rebel song and, well, some of the words were, ah, vulgar. I don't think she has any idea what they mean, of course. I just don't think these songs are appropriate, you know what I mean?"

"Actually, Sister I don't. I suspect she learned the song from my father and though I'd prefer she not use naughty words, I'd really have to know the lyrics to, ah, measure the offense."

Silence.

Pa told me never to sing his songs in school again. Well, he said, I could sing the harmless "McNamara's Band" but no rebel songs or funny songs.

He taught me more rebel songs. It seemed to bring him a sense of his lost country. If he couldn't dance anymore, he could still sing.

* * * * *

My grandfather wore the memory of Ireland like a pair of glasses that focused everything before him. Memory resists erasure of those parts of our youth where we once believed we could change the world. Ireland was the place he first committed himself to a cause beyond his farm boy's world of maggotted sheep, chickens who slept in the kitchen and teachers who'd slap you, while saying, "Your numbers, Murphy, your numbers!"

From a hill above the town of Castle Island, he looked over valleys splashed with chilled, soft rain. On rare sunny days, a glory of iridescent green farmlands shimmered in the distance. He had been born just after Britain permitted tenant farmers to buy the farms their ancestors had worked for Anglo-Irish landlords who, by the end of the 1800s, had come to own ninety five percent of Irish land. His father's family had been able to purchase their small farm, and he and his brothers had worked it until their father died.

Nothing in America could supplant the memory of that farm above Castle Island.

By fifth grade I was writing stories about the farm where Pa called the dogs in through the last spill of light fading across burnished hayricks, roads lined with hazel, hornbeam and gorse. I wrote about the rivers he named: the Caragh River with its "darlin salmon." He must have left for America in the late 1890s. My imagination was filled with County Kerry with its

80

MacGillycuddy's Reek mountain range and the Castle Island pubs where the young Denis danced all night.

Dinny loved Roosevelt but he was not passionate about America. He both desired and distrusted American acceptance. My parents, aunts, uncles...no one else had this conflict. They were Irish yes, and proud of it, but Americans. Even my grandmother was American. My grandmother, who was from West Meath between Athlone and Mullingar, said Ireland was a sad land with no central heating, bad weather, and too many men who looked backward, sang sentimental ballads, and drank.

"It's because you're not from Kerry," Dinny said.

"I've fed your thick Kerry men for years," she said. "They can dance, I'll give you that. Nothing else."

* * * * *

Dinny was my mother's music, too. She remembered the days of his dancing when he cleaned the black from his fingernails on Friday nights, rolled a keg of beer into the basement, set the chairs for Lynch the fiddler, Sullivan the accordionist, and Donahue the tin whistle player. He hummed as he carried the ham that Missus had cooked down the stairs into the basement ceili dance floor he'd fashioned by laying linoleum over the concrete slab of basement floor. Then the Kerry men and women arrived, boisterous and laughing. It was always his Kerry folks who came, rarely my introverted grandmother's Mullingar compatriots. Pa called the set dances, yelling out the foursome moves as the dancers swirled into reels and jigs. They stomped and high-kicked, keeping up with the fiddler's raging pace. Grey patches of sweat blottered the men's white shirts; the women's flowered dresses darkened where perspiration fanned out. The music carried them back and away from the work of shoveling and soot. Their music, so different from the big American bands, said everything they could not say. How America was full of promise, offered chances they could never have back home, how their children would surpass them. How grateful they were, how terribly sad, how far from home. They danced with fury for all that was lost.

* * * * *

The union was the family talk, the "pols" you could trust, the cowards and sell-outs "who forgot the people," the "boodle" Irish opportunists "who'd register dead people to vote for Hitler if he'd give their brother a job." Not that the union was idealistic. They never bucked the Chicago Irish political machine and patronage system. I don't know how the mob took kickbacks, but I know they did. My mother said it was more of a dues pay-off so they'd leave Pa's union to itself. The arrangements were shadow deals and none of my aunts knew how it all worked.

Perhaps the kickbacks to the mob began when my grandfather was chief boiler man at the Metropol Hotel where Al Capone lived. But it seemed that the mob had little interest in the fledgling Local#399 when Capone reigned at the Metropol. Capone gave the Irish janitor an odd, patronizing respect. Capone terrified Pa. He dreaded it when called from the hotel's black dust bowels to the mobster's gilded, red velvet suite.

The Metropol was festooned with brass spittoons, ferns, and plush sofas. There, in the midst of women patrons who wore sashes and sequins and the men wore fedoras, Dinny hurried to the back rooms, the basement. The hotel was a world apart for the Irish doorman, the porters, and the boiler men like my grandfather. A chasm gaped between the bawdy rich, the gangsters who controlled the $30 million a month in liquor sales, and the workers who served them.

Pa didn't want the union touched, so he deferred to Capone, carried his rosary to work, spoke of the priest of his parish, kept a distance. Capone left Dinny alone.

To the dapper crime boss, Denis Murphy was a worker in over-alls, a Mick, no threat at all. Still Capone respected his religiosity.

Though mostly invisible to Capone, Dinny did have one connection that interested the superstitious Al Capone. They were both Catholics. Capone thought Dinny Murphy was his one connection to God in the Metropol. No doubt Italian priests knew enough to stay away from the Capones. Capone called Pa to his room one day.

"Dinny," he said, " I've lost my rosary beads. I've asked St. Anthony, my paisan, to find them but maybe he's mad at me like the Bishops. Anyway, Murphy, you're a good Catholic, you may have the luck of your people. Find my beads."

Pa spent an hour on his hands and knees until he found the black beads Capone's mother had given him.

That evening Pa's son and four daughters gathered in a circle when he told the story. My mother said they all listened mesmerized. They cheered when Pa told them he found the beads.

"Then, by God, I found the damn rosary under a bed," Pa told them. "I was damn afraid not to, children. 'Good boy, Dinny.'" says he, like I am a child. But I am polite. I am always polite to that guy. I just want to leave the room."

My mother said Capone was charming, terrifying. He was a mad killer but Chicago itself was crooked. Pa accepted it as the American way. Besides Capone was a populist, tweaking the Chicago barons.

"When I sell liquor," Capone used to say, "they call it bootlegging. When my patrons serve it on silver trays on Lake Shore Drive, they call it hospitality."

* * * * *

Sixty years after the Republic Steel Memorial Day massacre, I went to a Memorial Day commemoration in the steelworker's union hall with my friend Allen Schwartz a labor songwriter. Across the street from the union hall a barely visible, faded sign read: *Republic Steel*. Behind the fence, industrial buildings were rusted and abandoned as old tractors dumped in fields. I stood facing the fields beyond the buildings, and I "saw" the cops close in on that Memorial Day, "saw" the chaos of bolting women and children, the slow flutter of fleeing boy's kites falling toward blood.

Then I walked across the street and entered the darkness of the hall where 50 white-haired men and a few women sat on folding chairs, staring at the stage waiting for the program to begin. The floorboards creaked when Ed Sadlowski, a labor leader when steelworkers were powerful and militant, walked onto the stage. Behind him a ratty red velvet curtain, hung in the robust years before the mills were closed, sagged.

"We'll never forget what happened here," Sadlowski said, and the men shifted in their chairs.

Then, Allen Schwartz walked on stage with his guitar. He said he was proud to be in a place where so much labor history was made. He said steelworkers were an inspiration. He asked them to sing with him. The old men barely hummed.

"Wait a minute," Allen said, "I was a kid when I read about the steelworkers and their struggles...I'm going to play "Solidarity Forever" and I want you all to sing and remember."

Then Allen ripped into the song, and one by one, those old guys in faded flannel shirts and shapeless suit jackets stood up and sang for a day long past when steelworkers had died to make a union. A number of them raised a fist.

After Sadlowski thanked them for coming and they shuffled toward card tables where they ate pizza for lunch. Soon it was time to leave. Someone opened the door and a shaft of sunlight lit the doorframe. They shook hands with each other, slipped on caps, and said good-bye. Then they walked through that illumined doorway into a May afternoon where, above Republic Steel, a cobalt sky blazed.

Kathleen O'Brien

Trajectory: Four Poems

Afternoons at Fourteen

It was my habit to pass through
the kitchen, grab a Ding-Dong
from the row of four Mom lined up
on the counter, dump my school books
on my bedroom floor and slip Victoria Holt
from under my pillow. I walked the mile
to the park, where under the orchard,
grass grew thick and tall
and smelled like honeyed apples.
Concealed behind that fertile curtain,
I settled my spine against tree bark ridges
and read, but mostly listened in
on the chatter of women walking in pairs
along the nearby path.

They talked of *he* and *him* and *them*
and *so mad* and *why do they*, and laughed.

Sometimes I altered the pattern,
greeted my mom in the kitchen,
told her I was going to Diane's
to study algebra and then hurried
down to the wash,
scaled the sagging cyclone fence,
descended the rusted iron rungs
stapled in the concrete wall. I followed
the captured creek's anemic trickle
to the tunnel that took it under the road,
where a boy waited. I lay on my back
on his lumpy denim jacket
as he felt about, touching places
I'd never even seen.
If I closed my eyes, I saw myself
water colored in pastel shades
upon a paperback.

Looking Back on Happy

On Fish Hatchery Road, morning glories and moonflowers
scaled the outside basement steps, and we admired this
but then one crept up a crack in the fireplace,
and Mom and Dad said flowers belong outdoors,
but Kathy wondered—do they?

Kittycorner across Eddie's and Jimmy's yard, Mr. Gerson
lit a bonfire in the fall. He threw in logs that snapped
like firecrackers and said it was termites exploding.
Pat wasn't sure, so Mr. Gerson showed us one, squirming,
and Eddie said Pat looked squirmy, too.

The mailbox was around the block, and on a mission
to drop a letter for Mom, Mike stubbed his big toe hard
and hopped and hopped then kept on walking
and left a speckled trail of big-toe blood, one dot
for every other step the whole way home.

Someone gave Sheila a second-hand Barbie,
blonde with blue eye shadow and lashes that blinked.
Kathy's gift was Barbie's pal Midge, perky and red-haired.
But Kathy's hair was blonde—Sheila had the red—
and the giving made no sense.

Out front, we circled the storm drain cover, darkening the sidewalk
with sweat that dripped from behind bent knees,
and shot marbles until just a little bit after
the voices of moms and dads compelled us in to safety.

What's It All About?

Amy sights her neighbor spying from his balcony as she leaves her apartment dressed in first-date gear. She almost flushes. She slept with the man for a couple weeks, then realized he was a loser, trying to replace his mom's tits with hers. But he still eyes her. This new guy drives his shitty car nearly an hour to take her to a nice place. He's polite for a while, but after they order, he seems to feel something has changed and starts asking personal questions. How many men have you done? How do you choose who you'll screw and who you won't? Did you pay for that sweater? because it looks really bad on you. *Holy fuck*, Amy thinks, *I don't even have cab fare home.* Why do you cut your hair like that? Has anyone ever mentioned you have no personality? Speechless, she stares. Why are you hiding your inner feelings? On the long ride home, she forces hollow thoughts, watches the ribbon of speckled blacktop through a floorboard hole. Back in her parking lot, she steps wordlessly out of the car, hesitates in lingering burnt-oil haze as taillights fade away. Tells herself, *It's not about me. It's not about me.* Once in her apartment, she changes into low, tight jeans and a tank top that shows off cleavage. Grabs two beers and knocks on her neighbor's door.

Why My Hair Grows Gray

One worn towel seizes fellow laundry
in every wash, loops loose ropy edge threads
around a sock, a sleeve, some hapless briefs,
and I question why I keep this rag
instead of giving it the toss.
Sometimes I think of its original burgundy,
my dramatic mismatched fancy,
but that richness is long gone,
oddly turned to pale burnt sienna—
and I blame the fading on some freak
bleaching incident. But then I recall
leaning down to smear blood
off the insides of pale thighs
from a midnight menstrual blowout,
relive the inelegant hands-and-knees pose
outside my child's bedroom to scrub
at peanut butter barf, summon up
nights spent dabbing a daughter's
tear-streaked mascara and mornings
over baby shit and puppy piss—
and the fading no longer mystifies,
seems like the natural thing.

Paul Dragavon

First Memory

The summer of 1938 was a busy one for my mother. She had four children. Dick, the youngest, was age two and still in diapers. I was three, Dennis was five, and Joan, six. In midsummer Dennis had to be rushed to St Mary's Hospital in Duluth a hundred and twenty miles south of Ely, due to kidney failure. Joan and I were confined to the yard to protect us from scarlet fever that was rampant among the children in the town.

More than seventy years have gone by since that summer and I still remember a dream I had in August...

In my dream, I awoke after a nap, and wandered out into the living room. As I walked through the house it seemed I was alone. The door to the basement was open and I went down the stairs. In the semi-darkness I could see the washing machine and hear the clothes swishing back and forth. Walking up to it I saw that it was no taller than I. The wringer was on and I reached over and let my fingers rub against the rollers. It felt so good letting them drag lightly as the rollers went around. I woke up. I didn't think anymore about the dream, nor did I tell it to anyone.

A day or two later I heard the washing machine running and went down into the basement. The cellar door to the outside was open and I could see my mother in the back yard hanging Dick's diapers. Remembering the dream, I walked over to the washing machine and saw that it was taller than it had been in my dream. I found a box to stand on but it wasn't high enough so I climbed onto the machine itself and hung on to the shaft. I held myself there with my left hand and reached over with my right to pull the lever to start the rollers, as I had seen my mother do. I touched the rollers lightly to feel that pleasant sensation I had dreamed about. Before I could feel anything my fingers were between the rollers and I couldn't get them out. Within seconds my hand was through the wringer, and as my arm was following I yelled for my mother.

Before she got to me the rollers were up to my elbow, which I kept bent so they couldn't get any farther up my arm. Mom rushed down the steps into the cellar, and quickly put the wringer in reverse. My arm and hand were freed. I started crying.

She carried me upstairs, laid me on their bed, and immediately phoned the doctor. Dr. Ayres came to the house. He thought my arm would heal okay, especially since the skin wasn't broken, but he noticed something more ominous. My temperature was well over a hundred degrees and he was certain that I was going to be part of an epidemic of scarlet fever that had been raging through town since the beginning of summer.

As he carried me out to his car he cautioned my mother, "Call if either of the other two children develop a fever, and be sure to wash the blankets that the little guy was lying on."

Dr. Ayres took me to Detention Hospital for Infectious Diseases, where those children, unfortunate enough to be caught up in the epidemic, were being treated.

As I lay there with scarlet fever my hand started to turn blue and black. A day or two later I awoke to find that when I moved my hand two fingers remained on my pillow. When my father came to visit that morning I told him about it and asked, "Am I going to come all apart?"

He assured me that I wouldn't, and told me, "Be a soldier. You know, they're brave, and they don't cry."

The next day, Dr. Ayres, observed the gangrene spreading and decided, in spite of my high fever, that it was necessary to operate. As they rolled me to the operating room, Dr. Ayres reminded me, "Be a good soldier, and if you don't cry I'll give you this lead soldier and this giant peppermint stick."

I tried not to cry, but couldn't hold back, as they moved me from the gurney to the operating table, and taped my arms down. I continued crying until the ether extinguished my consciousness and fear.

When I awoke the next morning my arm was gone. I couldn't see what had been done because of the big white bandage around the wound, but on the table next to my bed was the lead soldier and the giant peppermint stick.

Jane Hertenstein

Sense of Smell

Yesterday I was jogging past the hospital and paused, still running in place, waiting for the light to change. A waft of lilac drifted over to me.

One time in college I fasted for nine days. My intent was to rid the body of winter's impurities, cleanse my system of toxins.

After a few days of not eating, I was over being hungry. During the day I kept busy with classes, but in the evenings I was lost. Dinner was my transition time. I was used to sitting down before a plate or bowl and relaxing. I didn't know what to do with the extra time?

So to forget the emptiness inside of me I went for walks through neighborhoods. It was springtime finally after a dreary winter. The lilacs were in bloom. The fragrance was sweet, purple, reminding me of concord grapes. I stopped to inhale, my stomach ingesting itself. There was also honeysuckle in the air, which made me think of butterscotch.

I strolled past houses where I could tell someone was doing wash. Dryers vented lavender and warm roses through little pipes in the wall. It's a known fact that starving people—their senses heightened by the lack of food—have an especially acute sense of smell. The fresh smell of lavender-scented laundry detergent and lemon-fresh fabric softener drove me into primal paroxysms.

Trying to escape, I hurried further down the street until I was halted by the familiar odor of hamburger cooking and of onions sautéing. The intense late afternoon sun bounced bronze off the picture windows before me. My nose, fine-tuned by fasting, was able to detect the smell of fish, feathery flakes pulling away from filigree bones, smothered in melted butter, the color of custard, and garnished with parsley, more than a condiment, but an aesthetic, symbolizing rebirth, the greening of the world. I smelled bread fresh from the oven, bursting with tangy yeastiness, a soft springy sponge, steam rising, wafting, curling upward like invisible tendrils drawing me in. I swear I could smell red potatoes boiling, the zing of coarse salt, the brown scum foaming, roiling. Even the potato broth was intoxicating, possessing a bouquet, like a fine wine.

Suddenly I was transported back, the memory so real it seems three-dimensional: the five or six of us frying up boxes of batter-dipped shrimp, the crowded kitchen hazy with smoke, my t-shirt reeking of grease. I help by spreading out paper towel to soak up extra oil after Mom dumps a basket before refilling it. We eat in shifts, some of us standing, some of us sitting. Newspaper cones of steaming shrimp. My brother says sea horses are sexless, and I counter, no it's the men sea horses that have the babies. Serves them right says my older sister. We beg our mom for pop. She buys an 8-pack every week and rations it. Me and my sister are allowed to split a bottle. She pours and I choose—that way it's fair. Dad washes his shrimp down with beer. Pabst Blue Ribbon, the condensation sweating down the sides of the can. Bobo the cat, maddened by the smell, rubs against my ankles; through my bare feet I can feel her purring.

It was only a second. I awoke, embarrassed, a stranger hanging around outside other people's houses. I pushed on, hungrier than ever.

Then yesterday, at the corner of Clarendon and Marine Drive, I recalled that memory inside the other memory, both so far in the past as to have been buried in the margins of my mind. The light changed and yet I lingered, filled with longing.

Kevin Heath

Eat

Eat.

My cousin said breakfast for dinner is what alcoholic mothers serve their children.

Or if the mother gets a spinal injury and the dad has to make poached eggs and creamed peas forever.

She said breakfast for dinner is what you leave on the mercy table for the missionary family—canned pears nobody wants and Bisquick in a box so big it's got its own handle.

Our step-grandmother Doris stared at us like we were spider monkeys.

She said raise your hand if any child here has ever had to eat ketchup soup? Raise your hand if you ever had a onion pie?

No? Is it no then?

Eat your toast. Finish every last bite of those eggs. Tick-a-lock and eat.

"God, it's like we're orphan children," my cousin whispered.

"Or re-tarts," her sister whispered back.

Bethink

Kirk Wisland

A Stroke of Genius

You don't wind up trying to surf a midnight blizzard in the mountains outside Salt Lake City without jumping the guard rail or being run down by eighteen-wheelers, with only ninety dollars to try to make it from Vegas to Minneapolis in a terminally-ill baby-blue Honda Civic, with a newfound gambling addiction to add to an unmanageable debt, a suspended license, eight warrants for your arrest, no job, no cell phone to call for help and no health, car, or life insurance to pay for non-fatal repairs two days into the new Millennium with the lingering paranoia of nuclear reactor failure in the middle of missile silo and survivalist militia country, sporting an infected nose-ring and a bumper sticker that says *Jesus is coming, look busy!* without having made some questionable decisions in your life.

Martha Clarkson

Alterations

If you were a twelve-year-old girl in the seventies, you had to take Home Economics. In our class, I was the only one who didn't have a sewing machine at home, which also meant I was the only one who didn't have a sewing mother. She could do a button or a snap, and if she really pushed herself, darn a sock, but that was it. Maybe it was genetic, or maybe not, but I didn't want to sew either. I preferred to be outside, tossing my tennis ball on the roof over and over, practicing my hitting with a Whiffle bat and ball I pitched to myself. My little brother was never expected to learn to sew and could've been out in the backyard helping me improve my swing but he was obsessed with his violin. Wouldn't you know it, me, potential wunderkind of girls' softball, blessed with a brother who liked music more than sports.

Miss Montag, the Home Ec teacher, was definitely headed for spinsterdom, even though she couldn't have been over twenty-five. She had long black hair, freckles, and a pinched face that showed her distaste for us before we even did anything wrong. You could tell it was her first teaching assignment and you could also tell she could sew better than anyone ever hired at Butterick or Simplicity, the big pattern makers.

The machines were lined up under the row of windows in the classroom of the old school. If you looked out those windows, which I preferred to do rather than confront the sewing assignment we were being lectured on, you could see the woodshop building. Inside, the boys were hunched over the machines looking like a union operation without the coveralls. It was where I wanted to be. That fall it was warm enough to have the windows open in both rooms and the screech of the table saw was the music I wanted to hear, not the muffled chug of sewing machines. Girls weren't allowed to take shop —for heaven's sake, we'd just been allowed to wear *pants* —but the PTA was voting on it at the next meeting. My fingers were perennially crossed. I would've sewed them together if I'd known how.

The first assignment was to make an apron for our mothers. Really, that's how Miss Montag said it. As if it was an impossibility for a father to cook, though mine made a better pancake than iHop. My mother took me fabric shopping and I selected a blue Aztec-ish print that she said "could be awfully busy on the eyes." I held out.

Kristee Lufwah was the top sewer in our class. She was so good that she garnered special dispensation from Monty, as we'd taken to calling Miss Montag, by completing a sewing test that required her to install a zipper and blind stich a hem. This gave her the freedom to sew whatever she wanted. "The apron is too simple for me," she said, when one of us first noticed she was over in the corner cutting out fabric from a complicated pattern, a plaid fabric to boot, which she'd assured Monty she knew how to match. "I made aprons in first grade," she said. Her mother was renowned for her sewing, because Kristee wore only home-sewn clothes, and they were the envy of the girls in our grade. If only I'd had a mother who sewed, I'd have inherited the talent just by sharing the same house with her and wearing the clothes she made me, which would be the cutest in the school. How could you avoid understanding how a dirndl skirt went together if you had half a dozen in your closet?

Some of the machines were new and some not, and we all wanted the new ones because they had a 'slow' setting, and because the fight for them turned vicious at one point – hair-pulling, tripping – Monty made us draw straws. Mine was short. The old black Singer I was assigned to I shared with Tracy Pullman, a girl with a big nose who also wore homemade clothes, but you could tell, because the hems were crooked and the sleeves different lengths. But I couldn't make fun of her because she had a sewing machine at home, and a sewing mother, and maybe she'd even made those clothes herself, in which case a crooked hem was understandable. She sat right down at the Singer as if it was her own and threaded the machine without asking for help. I stood by the window and watched the woodshop – not because I liked boys, because I liked woodworking. Or the thought of it.

"Caroline," Monty would say to me, "come back to the table to cut out your fabric." And she said the end of my name LINE, when I called myself Caro*linn*. I scuffed over – because I wanted the scuffing of my saddles to indicate how much I didn't want to sew the apron and maybe get to bake a ham or dinner rolls instead – she'd add, "Creating an apron is making something too." That was because I had voiced my opinion about wanting to be in woodshop, *making something*. And more than once I'd said it, loud, which I sometimes could be.

Tracy threaded my blue spool into the machine for me when Monty wasn't looking, and then I sat in the posture of a sewer, which I'd carefully observed. The bright white lamp on the machine was lighting up the needle and presser foot that looked to me like a vicious little monster ready to eat my fabric, and possibly my finger. My foot hovered over the pedal on the floor but I just couldn't bring myself to press down on it. Visions of crooked seams danced in my head.

I stood up and did a kind of jig along the row of machines, singing "Strike three, ball four, a walk, a run'll tie the score. Fly ball, double play, Yankees win again today!" These were lyrics from *Damn Yankees*, my favorite musical. Who didn't want to sing about baseball? And my voice was pretty good. "Those damn Yankees, why can't we beat 'em?" Then the hard part, marching to each machine as I went back and forth with the lyrics: "He's out, he's safe, he's out, he's safe, he's out, he's safe, he's out!" The next lines were about how blind the ump was, but I didn't get to sing them because Monty was in front of me, the sewing machines had stopped, and she was close enough I could see the black mustache hairs she'd attempted to bleach.

The principal's office was baby blue, which didn't fit the facial expressions of Mr. Newton, fondly known among us at Newty-the-Patooty, and his chiseled expression of impatience. Apparently 'damn' wasn't on the list of acceptable words for elementary school. My mother sure used it a lot.

I tried to explain to Newty that I didn't like to sew, and that woodshop would be a much better fit for me, and maybe put in a good word to influence the PTA vote coming up. "I am very well-suited to being a laborer," I said in my deep voice, a practiced imitation of Sidney Poitier, when he says this to his cotton field boss in *Something of Value*. I don't think Newty got the reference, which meant he was probably a racist and didn't like black actors.

"Caroline, sewing is part of any woman's life. An apron is a glorious thing. Embrace it. Don't disgrace the splendor of home economics, a *very scientific* field, by using expletives." He looked over the rim of his glasses without softening his expression. Mrs. Canfield, his busy-body secretary, came in as if on cue and said, "Now, now my dear, back to class we go. Remember, learning to sew your own clothes will make you that much more attractive to a man when the time comes. We must prepare all aspects of home management." She escorted me out and insisted on going all the way back to Monty's room with me. On the way, she extoled the virtues of Jello, how she learned to make party favors with yellow Kleenex, and the importance of aprons. I wondered if she knew the words to *New Rochelle* from the musical "How to Succeed," where the young secretary just wants to be a housewife – *I'll be so happy to keep his dinner warm..."* It made me sick, that song, even though I liked the rest of the show, especially the old company president who wears the huge beaver coat and waves a Yale pennant around during his big number.

The needle on the old Singer didn't eat my fabric, or stab my finger, and Tracy even conceded to helping me out when it came to pushing the apron's tie through a channel with a safety pin on one end, a concept I never really got. In between starting the project and Tracy's help, I pretended I lost a pattern piece but Monty was onto me and had extras. I hid the fabric for the pocket so maybe I could take a test on paper or something instead of finishing (getting the pocket on straight was a big grading item), and feigned a sore throat by showing how I couldn't even sing. After the aprons were done, Tracy told me that Monty had asked her to stay after one day and enlisted her to help me sew the apron. Tracy sewed her own pocket on crooked but she still got an A on the project. Because she was helping me, my pocket was sewed on crooked too. My ties were uneven lengths, and I got a C, but the Aztec fabric looked swell, like we were about to grind corn on the mesa. I gave it to my mom and she wore it when she put TV dinners in the oven.

That fall they approved girls to take wood shop and boys to take home ec. Who signed up first? Besides Geoff Linden and his anklets signing up for home ec, me. That got me out of the cooking part of Monty's year and into table saws and drill presses. Mr. Cramer, the old-goat who ran the shop, made us take a test on each piece of equipment and showed us a film strip of kids who'd lost fingers and eyes due to ignoring safety practices. Then he asked us to draw our design before we could make it. I pored over that blank newsprint for days. Lisa Preacher was the only other girl, an eighth grader, and she apparently had a woodworker father, because she got special dispensation to build a parson's table, which was the mod style then and complicated even though it was entirely square. I saw how much easier it was to have a pattern to work from and I asked Crame-O if he had any.

"This is about *your* creations, Caroline," he said, and pronounced it LINE, like Monty had. I must've done something to make them want to be so long-voweled with my name.

I couldn't think of anything to make, so I copied a pair of candlesticks Ricky Slee was turning on the lathe. Cramer told me the lathe was hard but I liked the image of bending over that spinning machine, sawdust flying. The part I forgot was that a pair of candlesticks has to match and the two I produced from some laid-up scraps of ash Cramer had looked nothing alike. I got a C and gave them as Christmas presents to people in separate households.

The next year I tried out for the chorus, which was required if you wanted to be in the spring musical. *Oklahoma!* had never seen such talent.

Adina Ferguson

Writers Don't Lie

People don't lay they lie. I don't lie. I just choose not to answer my phone. My phone vibrates and I look at the caller. I hope they choose not to leave a voicemail but they do anyway. I don't leave voicemails because I hate my voice. I'm insecure like that. I chose to use the word insecure because I didn't feel like spelling self conscious and I didn't know which form of the word to use. You know, "conscious" or "conscience." I have a Bachelor of Arts in English. People remind me of that when I say something grammatically incorrect. I remind my family the same thing as I beat them in some game called "Words With Friends. I'm addicted, I'll admit. But I also am a Blackberry user. The two don't go together so I have to settle on the Facebook application via my Dell. I don't own a Mac or an I-product except iTunes. I don't own an Android. I should get paid for all this product placement. I learned about product placement in high school. My class was forced to watch our teacher's favorite movie "Cooley High." It's a black movie from the 70's. Though I was born in the 80's, I enjoy too. That same teacher and I are friends on Facebook. I found out her ex-husband was a musician in a group back in the day. I'd use the word "famous" but I had never heard of the group. She's a writer, though I've never read any of her work. Doesn't mean she too isn't famous. Right now, neither am I though I'm "googable." For now, I work at a University doing things I can't describe to common folks. Now that, I wish I could lie about that.

Guinotte Wise

Slouching Towards Horsmanship

Horses have informed most of my life. They've owned me for more than half that hefty span. Being without them is not a reality to me. There have been at least fifty over the years, but about ten I remember vividly. I am not a trainer, nor am I, in any sense, an accomplished horseman. I have friends who are and, in this area, I'm sure they look down upon me in a rueful manner, shaking their wise heads.

I've had quarterhorses (mainly), drafts, apps, grade horses, a Mexican Galliceno, Pasos, walking horses, foxtrotters, appendix-breds, saddlebreds, ponies, in every color of the equine rainbow. Each one had a unique personality. Each one taught me something about life and about myself. Their teaching methods were varied but fell mainly into one of two camps: The "Bad things happen fast" method, and the "Don't do that again" method. Often the two were combined. I've been kicked, bitten, rolled on, dragged, chased, bucked off, run off with, tree branched and humiliated. I always came back for more.

I wanted one of those furry little Icelandic horses but found none available in Kansas. I had an outlaw paint draft horse shipped in from Nova Scotia by way of Kentucky, so anxious to be trampled am I. At great expense, I might add. Gentle giants, I was told. I was also told, in high school, that the cops couldn't chase you across the state line. I exploded both myths dramatically.

My relations with horses, as I've hinted, are not sound in the eyes of friends who are horse people. I once bought a Shetland pony, (that should make me suspect to even the rookiest of horse fanciers) even though I had a herd of eight or nine regular-sized horses. He was an agile little guy and could kick a large horse in the gut if pushed. He felt pushed often, being of cranky disposition. The other horses avoided him like rats are said to scram from sinking ships.

I bought him for my small children but he didn't like them. He liked me. Mr. Walker was his name and we had a game that possibly had its beginning after I'd had a few pops. I'd get on him, bareback. He'd buck me off over his head. I'd land on my feet. He'd wait patiently for me to get on him again. This could go on a long time. I never reached his limit for this but mine was about ten minutes. Then, as I was walking away he'd thunder up behind me, slam on the brakes and butt me with his head. I'd throw my arms out and pitch forward, running crazily, and he'd think that was fine. Once he did that when it was muddy and he slid right over me. He actually seemed apologetic.

It's dangerous to anthropomorphize most animals we are told, but we are also taught to do so by Disney movies and all the other Pixar propaganda poured into our souls from birth. At our Wise Compound, dogs talk and horses conspire. Toads live in mansions. It's a magical place where I slip back into childhood.

The horse obsession started early for me. I was way too young to know or care that horses attracted girls, but I became aware of this in high school and it added to my rationale. In fact, between marriages, it fueled the rationale.

I was a melodramatic child; I see this now as I look back. Nothing will distance you from parents and the world at large so much as stagecraft and idiocy packed into one. I rolled eyeballs back into foreheads like a laudenum overdose. I came by these histrionics historically, genetically. Much of the family had been artists, poets, politicians, opera-involved. Moody little French fur trapper forebears peered into campfires and saw their madness. One great uncle chased people about with his sword cane. Another did donuts on Missouri River ice in a 1938 Dodge automobile. All drank. Most were horse-owners, some were ranchers. It was as though I was coached, little cheering sections of DNA hollering approval of over-the-top behavior. Denied a Daisy BB gun, I didn't mope. I quit eating. I held my breath. I penned my obituary. Eyeballs rolled.

When I was a kid in Tulsa, maybe nine, I cried myself into hiccup spasms under the back porch on weekend nights, with only Susie the old springer spaniel for company. She was my stepfather's duck dog. The reason for my inconsolable distress, of course, was I desperately wanted a horse. This need went unrequited and unremarked. Even Susie slunk away.

I pleaded with my parents who, I see now, were somewhat sardonic anyway and had little patience for overwrought kids. My stepfather did one of his "I'll take care of this," hiking-his-pants moves and took me to a rancher acquaintance, had him put me up on a high-powered cutting horse who dumped me early on, being used to knee signals that conflicted with whatever I was doing. A calf darted up out of a draw and I was airborne.

The long fall to the hard ground knocked the wind out of me, and gave my old man to say, "Maybe we don't want a horsie after all, huh boy?" I sullied up and was quiet on the ride home, noting his smirk from time to time, having disposed of another annoying quirk from his inherited weird-acting kid. No deal. I had been on a handsome creature and would climb aboard many more.

My first real love, my high school sweetheart, had a horse. Was that the reason we were so entwined? I don't think so, no I *know* that's not the reason. She was a green-eyed, raven-haired beauty. It was a combination of chemicals, physical attraction and that collision of pheromones that afflicts teens, plus something indefinable but unmistakable people call love. With all this going on, it's a miracle that I even graduated.

Her horse, Midnight, a rangey, ribby character, was stabled at a Kansas City establishment that still exists; Benjamin Stables. We rode together on the picturesque trails there. I participated in their rodeos some time later, after this girl and I had taken vastly different forks in the road. In college I found time, between classes and working at Miller's 66 station, to locate a riding/boarding stable. This was at Westminster, in Fulton, Missouri.

At any rate, I married a horsewoman while still in college, and it wasn't long before we'd found a way to own horses, both of us possessing a similar indifference to facts and life lessons. Like a lot of young horsey fools, we felt that, with enough horses, we could make money on them! Start a business! Board and train! Buy and sell!

If I were a banker and an earnest couple with similar intentions came to me with such a plan, I'd laugh them out the front door. In a hurry. And don't come back! I have never seen a horse operation succeed. Other than those big money racing stables, and I suspect they cover up negative cash flow *hemorrhages* with infusions from various trusts and foundations as Byzantine as the casino business.

* * * * *

But there was one horse out of all the others that was magic. He spoiled me for all time, made me think that I was some kind of natural horseman, pumped my ego way up, and became, in a very short time, my partner. His name was Thor when I first laid eyes on him. God of war. And he did look somewhat like a war horse. Roman nose, roched mane, ass end like a boxcar, muscled front, feathered hoofs. Thor was a buckskin who came to Iowa from Arizona and had been a hazing horse, from what sketchy information anyone could pass along about him. He was maybe twelve, a grade horse with some Percheron to him, big, husky, built like an oversized foundation quarter horse. He was beautiful. I first saw him as a head jutting out of a barn window-hole. He looked like a Frazetta comic book horse—something Death Dealer might ride into a horde of Mongols as he finished them off.

I had been advised Thor was for sale, the price being $250. I committed to him without seeing any of the rest of him. That magnificent head was it for me. Fortunately, the rest of him was commensurate. I approached the barn and talked to him, and was, in turn, approached by his owner. What followed was one of the weirdest horse-oriented conversations I've ever experienced.

"You want something?" Not a welcoming tone.

"Yeah, this horse is for sale I understand?"

"To the killers. I'm sellin' him for dog meat."

"Uh, why would that be?"

"Sumbitch drug me on a gravel road."

"How much the killers paying for him?"

"Don't care. They can have him for free." Back in those days the renderers paid $100 or more for a horse. Now, you have to pay them.

"But I'll pay more than they will."

"Don't care. Want him dead." This person had been drinking fairly heavily and it was only about 10am on a Saturday morning. At that time of my life I was a drinker, but, like a lot of lushes, didn't start until noon. That way, I felt I had control over it. I didn't, of course, but it's beside the point here. I'd heard this guy was a knee-walking, snot-flying lush and that he mistreated this horse and various other animals. He'd lost his license and now used Thor as transportation to a downtown bar, where he tied him in the alley until such time as he rolled out of the bar and rode him home. Apparently on one of these homecomings, Thor's owner had slipped sideways and been dragged along, probably at a walk judging from the fact he was still with us.

I changed the subject and pretended to leave.

"Nice meeting you, Tom" I lied. "It was a pleasure."

"Yeah. Stop by for a beer sometime." He gestured at the barn. Maybe he lived there.

"Sure will," I lied again.

"Hell, have one now." He ducked into the barn and returned with two wet cans fresh from an ice filled cooler, popped one, gave me the other. We drank, smoked, talked about the difficulties of living one's own life without being jacked around by various authorities and bluenoses. Then the subject of Thor came up.

"You want that horse."

"Yes, I'd like to have him all right."

He appeared to be on the verge of sullenness again, thought for a moment, said, "You can have him if you take him right now."

"Do you have a saddle and bridle I can borrow?"

"I don't loan out tack. Do I look like a fucking moron?" Yes, I wanted to answer. And butt ugly, too.

"Well, how can I take him right now?"

"That's your problem. I need $250 cash money."

Fortunately I'd brought just that and handed it over. He counted it twice. Meantime, I searched around the outside of the barn and came up with some baling twine and a green piece of branch which I cut with a pocketknife. I had never tried this before but fashioned a bit out of the stick and attached the twine to both ends, tied another piece of twine around the rig and Thor's nose to stabilize it after I'd fitted the bit in his mouth. I led him to a good sized rock and hoisted myself up on his back fully expecting him to cut loose on me once I got aboard. Nothing. He stood quietly. Even Tom seemed taken aback. He had opened another beer without offering me one, and sat with his back against the barn, scowling as though he'd been taken advantage of.

"I'll be back for my car," I said. Without waiting for an answer, I wheeled Thor around and to the tractor path that led to the gravel road. I gave him a little touch in the ribs with my heels and he jigged up to a fast trot which I slowed to a walk. I had maybe two miles to go with a major highway to cross on the journey. There was no drama on the trip. It was as though the horse and I had been a duo forever. I renamed him Percy on the way to celebrate his obvious Percheron heritage, and I talked to him constantly. We had to use the median of the highway for a quarter mile, and the passing trucks and cars didn't seem to bother him beyond a naturally intelligent wariness. When we rode through a residential area, dogs didn't spook him, but I felt him bunch up a little if one got close, preparatory to kicking if he needed to.

We finally arrived at his new home, Porky Dexter's pig farm, where a group of us had rented a house and a barn and installed a personable young man to oversee it. We called the place Lazy Frank's Dirt Farm. Percy took to it. I put him in a holding pen and watched him while I waited for someone to show up and take me to my car. That was the start of an amazing sixteen-year relationship, one that made me think all horses were very special animals. Many weren't. Percy was.

I was a drinker back then. Percy didn't like Tom, his former owner, and I thought that dislike and mistrust would ignite if I ever approached Percy with a snootful. The very smell of alcohol would mask the fact that I had good intentions. I needn't have worried. He did everything he could to stay underneath me.

Nobody else could ride Percy. Lazy Frank tried and gave up. Percy didn't like women we discovered. He'd back through a three-rail fence with a female on his back. He only acted normal with me on him. I say normal; he had his predilections.

Once, a police car stopped us at about 3am, and the driver informed me that in that Iowa county any moving conveyance was required to have a red light to the rear. "Shoot, did that thing go out again?" I said, and they threw gravel, laughing upon departure. Percy was bunched and ready to do damage to the vehicle, but I held him in. Blitzed as I was I knew better than to vandalize public property.

The spirits (Jack Daniels and a host of night shapes) moved me to ride late at night. It felt like freedom. Percy and I would range here and there, through pastures, over hill and Indian burial mound, or so we would conjecture, gathering up what spirits awaited in the inky night, canter down roads we knew, discover byways. I would sing at the top of my voice; usually the song was "Hooley-ann" and I would put Percy's name in place of "Ol' Paint" and whenever his name came up his ears would stand at attention. "I ride an ol' Percy, I lead an ol' Dan, I'm goin' to Montana to throw the Hooley-ann. Ol' Bill Jones had a daughter and a son, son went college and the daughter went wrong, wife got killed in a poolroom fight and still he keeps singin' from mornin' to night." And we would ride into the night, sleep and the job be damned.

My own gravel road situation came up on one of these rides. Percy, like a lot of horses, bloated a bit when you'd cinch him up, thereby loosening the cinch strap afterward, for comfort's sake. Usually I would compensate for this by cinching it a hair tighter. Not this time. I dimly recall hoisting myself up on him and falling off the other side. He stood quietly, craning his neck to watch this spectacle. Finally I was aboard and we began another night adventure.

I must have "fallen asleep" as we say in the program, and something went haywire. It was a gravel road, and I was, shoulder to gravel, upside down, my feet caught in the stirrups—the saddle had slipped underneath his belly. I said whoa, and Percy stopped. Perhaps he was already stopped. This situation would have been perilous on any other horse in the universe. He watched with a gracefully curved neck while I worked at getting one foot out, then the other. I had hold of one rein and lost that in the process.

I fell beneath him with a thump, watching his four legs. I stood shakily, gathered the reins, leaned against his warm shoulder and thanked him over and over. I righted the saddle, cinched it snugly, and we rode back home. I have never forgotten that incident, testimony to friendship and patience of a horse who had little patience for other horses, people, automobiles, or blowing leaves. Yet he stood for me. He put up with me. What streamed through my mind as I hung below him, was how Tom, the other lush, had been dragged on a gravel road. Was I to suffer the same fate? I deserved it, no doubt in my mind. I even accepted it to a degree. Thank God and Percy for mercy. A hoof in the head would have ended things right then and there.

In the next fifteen years we moved from Iowa to Wisconsin, then back to Kansas, and Percy was always there. In Wisconsin, we had a neighbor with a green tennis court, and he called from time to time to say Percy was on it. It was a hard court, so we never learned what his attachment to it was; he just liked standing on it. Across the road was the Milwaukee Country Club, and Percy and his good friend Senor would sometimes join the golfers, who played through the grazing duo. Sixteen years with an antic a day is a lot of material. This horse was one in a million.

Ernest Seton Thompson said the last chapter in an animal's life is always a tragedy, and so it was with Percy, as he began to lose his sight and invulnerability. We figure his life span was in the 30's and he certainly showed unmistakable signs of enjoying most of it hugely. But he taught me things. And he showed me things about myself that I shied away from, and later managed to confront. Who knows, maybe his dignity will show up in me some day.

Jared Duran

The Drunk and the Drink

What came first, the drink or the drunk? Do I drink because I am a drunk, or do I drink to get drunk? I suppose I look at the answer in this way: The latter is the inevitable result of drinking (assuming that this is the desired effect), whereas the former is the embodiment of a lack of ability to control the desire for the state of the latter. I like to look at the answers to questions I don't like in a long-winded fashion inspired by dodgy logic—it helps me sleep nights.

That's not really true though. Anyone that has known me for any length of time can attest to the fact that if there are questions I don't like, I simply don't answer them. I'm a great believer in the power of avoidance. If you ignore something long enough, it eventually goes away, right?

That, of course, isn't really true either.

Let us go backwards a bit.

My father was a drunk. He was also abusive. I recall the paddle he used on me as a child—it was a wooden job with holes in it. Whether the holes were for extra emphasis, speed, making an interesting pattern on my ass, or merely decorative, I was never sure, but it hurt like hell. His weapons of choice were his hands, which he used liberally anywhere that couldn't be seen in public. I know that during their marriage, my mother was the focus of his abuse—something that I believe stemmed from deep-seated insecurity, jealousy, and fear that she might leave him. She eventually did leave him when I was four, but my brother and I were forced to see him for some time after that. That's when the focus of his violence shifted mainly to me, although my brother got a taste of it as well. I'm not sure what this stemmed from. Maybe there was some jealousy of us as well. Maybe he was simply lacking some internal mechanism that tells the rest of us, "Hey, don't hit your kids, numb nuts." My mom says that she used to look forward to my father getting drunk, because he was at his most pleasant. I've spent my entire life concerned that I will become my father.

I started drinking at home when I was fairly young. This was completely sanctioned by my mom. Her rationale being if I were able to drink in a safe environment without any sort of stigma attached to it then I would not be tempted to sneak around and experiment out there in the big unknown. I think that I was around ten when I began to partake of the Manischewitz at family gatherings and holiday dinners. I can't touch the stuff anymore—way too sweet. At around fifteen or so I was allowed to have some real wine, and beer was alright. I don't remember exactly when, but by the time I moved out of the house, I was allowed to grab a beer whenever I felt like it. I'm not so sure that this did me any good. I took to alcohol like a morbidly obese man takes to Twinkies.

I've never had any faith in AA. I went to a meeting once with a roommate, and I couldn't identify with the people there. I received a call at work one day saying that I needed to go home because said roommate, after having a bad crystal meth experience, thought he heard people trying to break into the apartment and had called the police. Not that I needed any additional reason to dismiss AA, but there it was. Many people have great success with AA, and I don't mean to discount that. However, I don't go around telling people how to live their lives, so...

I got married when I was nineteen. This piece is not going to be about that, but it does tie in somewhat to my drinking. It was shortly after I got married that I entered a period where I was drunk more often than not. Dana, my ex-wife, is bipolar, and this, no joke, played a large part in the ups and downs of our marriage. About two years into our marriage we split, and I slept on a recliner in my friend Alec's studio apartment for a few months. I'm pretty sure that I was drunk almost every night I lived there. I vividly recall spending my 22nd birthday in that apartment alone, making my way through a large container of Smirnoff apple flavored vodka. The stuff tasted terrible, but once I started to feel the effects, it really didn't matter. I tested a lot of friendships during this period, and the strongest ones held while others faded and fell away.

Drinking became a way for me to exorcise a lot of what I couldn't bring myself to talk about when I was sober. With Dana, I had some of my most unguarded moments when I was plastered. We got back together after being separated for a year—a big mistake on my part, and then split for good some two years after that. At the end of our relationship, she took everything I had told her in these moments of vulnerability—my concerns, fears, problems with my family, and threw them right in my face. This sent me crawling straight back into the bottle, and any progress I'd made towards trusting people was completely lost. It is wrong to take advantage of someone who has opened up and put their trust in you. That is something that would never occur to me in a million years.

Still, drinking isn't all bad. I've had some great ideas while I was drunk. Some of my most honest pieces of writing have come out of a state of inebriation. That doesn't make drinking any less self-destructive, and it's not a good reason to start. Chris Difford of the band Squeeze wrote some of the greatest lyrics ever put to paper while he was drunk, but it also did irreparable damage to his life and relationships with his loved ones. He eventually had a breakdown, went through support groups and retreats, and has never really been the same since. I don't want that to be me. This is only one man's opinion, but I consider not being able to work through your own problems a weakness, and I have to live with me, so... As I sit here writing this, these lines from Yeats' "A Drunken Man's Praise of Sobriety" keep rolling around in my head, "A drunkard is a dead man/And all dead men are drunk."

In 2006, amidst the rubble of my crumbling marriage, I met Adrianna. Again this piece isn't about my relationship with Adrianna, but it does go a long way towards explaining my present relationship with the bottle. I wasn't looking for any sort of long term relationship. In fact, I thought in the wake of the mess of the last five years I was due for a bit of fun. Well, I got the fun, but I also got one of the most rewarding, fulfilling, functional (not a dirty word—in actuality, much preferred to dysfunctional) relationships of my entire life. I've received no end of shit from friends that she's ten years older than I am and has three kids to boot. Here's where I stand on the subject of love: You don't choose who you fall in love with. There's a clear difference between simply finding somebody attractive, and actually loving/being in love with somebody. It's a feeling that's hard to describe, but when you have it you just know it, and you'd better follow it—whether or not it works out, or you'll regret it. I've done all three. I fell in love with Dana, and it turned out to be a disaster. I fell in love with Claire (which I'm not going to delve into at all here) while I was split from Dana the first time, but I chalked it up to a manifestation of the nearly constant drunken stupor I was in at the time, and I've always regretted it. Thankfully, I followed my heart with Adrianna, and it's the best decision I've ever made.

Since then, my drinking has certainly been curbed. I've had a desire to deal with things in a more constructive way, and I can't say that I haven't had the urge to make a mad dash for the nearest bottle, and I can't say that I haven't given into that urge on more than one occasion, but it's like Leonard Cohen said, "I fought against the bottle, but I had to do it drunk." The thing is that I still like to drink, certainly in social settings, but, more than likely due to all the drinking I've done over the years, I have to drink a ridiculous amount to get that nice buzz going. My drink of choice for a while was Jack Daniels, and I've sort of lost my taste for that, which is alright.

Over the years, I've developed a habit I would have chastised others for not so long ago: When I hear kids (twenty-one seems so young and long gone to me now) talking about how they're gonna go get plastered, wasted, or blotto, I feel an overwhelming urge to lecture them on the dangers and long-lasting effects such a thing can have on them—it makes me feel ridiculously old, but then a lot of decisions I've made in my life have had the effect of making me feel a lot older than I am, and I find myself growing increasingly impatient with impetuous youth. I imagine myself shaking my fist at them and making snide, sarcastic remarks like one of the old guys in the balcony of The Muppet Show.

To drinking! To all the wonderful things and terrible disasters that ensue. (Writer raises bottle of Guinness to lips and takes deep pull—more now because he likes the taste than for any sort of effect it is likely to have on his evening.)

Fran Tempel

The Jewelry Box

Montana winters in the early 1950's were agonizingly cold with temperatures often falling below zero for days or weeks on end. The constant wind drove iciness through the bones and stabbed at the heart. Often, very often in fact, the bitter winters of my youth were accompanied by snowfalls measured in feet not inches. It wasn't uncommon to venture out into a world of white with snow banks four or more feet high. Icicles were huge! In an old photo I am holding one so large I have to cradle it in both arms as if carrying a stack of wood! Thermometers weren't necessary: we could tell the temperature by the way the snow crunched or the way it appeared to be sprinkled with millions of glittering diamonds or even the way the hairs in our noses stuck together. Snowsuits existed but we were without the financial means to purchase such a luxury. The key was to layer, layer, layer. And it was still cold.

Those in the family who were daring enough to brave the elements for pure enjoyment spent time outside playing Fox and Geese, building snow forts for scheduled snowball fights and, when they were so wet that plopping down in the snow could do no additional damage, delighted in making snow angels . Then in they would come, don dry clothes and attempt to find other forms of amusement. I was content sitting in front of the tall living room stove reading and dreaming about the characters I met in each novel as if they were old friends.

There was only one activity that would entice me to spend time out in what I considered to be the frozen wasteland. My two older sisters and I would venture out, if the snow wasn't too deep to handle, and go door-to-door offering to shovel sidewalks. The oldest, Kathy, age twelve, had the shovel, the middle sister Helen, age ten, carried the ice chipper while I, age eight, had the broom. Our fee was $1.00 from steps to street for a job done to the neighbor's satisfaction. Often we would receive a much appreciated generous tip. We would arrive home tired, warmed by the exertion, elated by the extra spending money that Mom wouldn't have to supply. Montana had no paper money in those days so the mere heft of silver dollars and fifty cent pieces made us feel rich. Counting out the take I often felt like Silas Marner -- so intent on the importance of money. It meant independence.

Having no television to take our minds off the claustrophobic atmosphere of the season, we spent a great deal of time listening to radio programs such as *Inner Sanctum Mysteries* which terrorized us; *The Jack Benny Show* which made us laugh; *The Grand Ole Opry* which joined us as a chorus and The Lone Ranger which instilled in us a sense of fair play and justice. We had countless library books to devour; jigsaw puzzles to assemble, pillow cases and tablecloths to embroider, socks to darn, cards to play and games we would invent on the spur of the moment. But, there came a time when the winter was just too unbearable and no amount of diversions would cure what Mom referred to as "Cabin Fever."

If anyone could find a way to bear impossible situations it was our mother.

Here was a woman experienced in forbearance. Widowed at the age of forty-three; five months pregnant with her tenth child. Three grown children on their own; now a single parent caring for her five girls and two boys. Her mother struggled with Parkinson's for years, Mom acting as caretaker. Mom, herself had had a brush with polio; experienced the influenza of 1918 when she was ten which took the lives of family members, friends and neighbors. Her favorite sister died prematurely of cancer; most recently our dad felled by a heart attack at the age of fifty. It was little wonder that she was overly protective; anxious about potential harm befalling her family. Behind her back we laughed at some of her maxims, but her belief was so strong - as she was - that none dared contradict her.

Many of these gems merely annoyed us: Don't sit on the ground in the early spring or you will get polio; don't let an empty rocking chair stay in motion or it would bring sickness to the family; cracking one's knuckles would cause rheumatism just as walking outside with wet hair would bring on a cold. Then the ubiquitous: Always wear clean underwear and carry a hankie in case one was, for some inexplicable reason, taken to the hospital. These words of wisdom were, after all, "for our own good." Consciously she made efforts to direct us toward physical health. Unconsciously the most important underrated gems she provided were a sense of imagination and wonder, which contributed to our emotional strength. It is because of her that we were all avid readers, first listening to her read to us, discussing the story afterward and then later delving into our own novels, sharing them with each other. Reading opened our eyes to possibilities beyond the confines of our home, our town, our state.

So it was with the onset of "Cabin Fever" she came to our rescue.

The two boys, being older, usually found an outlet at a friend's house or some other form of entertainment which left the five younger girls tired of the puzzles and other traditional means of passing the time. Hearing the inevitable bickering beginning to take on some intensity, Mom would leave the sanctuary of her sewing room, calmly join us in the front room, sit in her favorite rocking chair, and announce "I think I should organize my jewelry box". Akin to the words "Open Sesame," they filled us with a glow of anticipation. One of us would excitedly volunteer to bring the box to her. Like an altar boy delivering the bible to the priest or Christopher Columbus presenting the Queen of Spain with newly discovered treasures, the messenger advanced, delicately placing the case in her lap. The remaining four girls gathered around her chair, resting elbows on the arms or pulling up a footstool to get a better view. There was a tacit agreement in our home that this container was sacred. No one dared look inside without expressed permission; it was the one bit of privacy of which our mother was assured. Besides, Mom was the wizard and the magic of the box would be rendered impotent had she not been there to orchestrate our journey.

As she lifted the lid on the white case, a two-tier tray moved to the fore. Its white satin lining was embedded with minute embroidered stars; the numerous soft red velvet compartments made each piece of costume jewelry appear rich and majestic. Her small graceful hands would reach inside as she tickled the necklace strands, broaches and earrings until she decided where to begin. At the point of her selection, the voyage commenced. Taking the article in her hand, she would embark upon the genesis of the piece: who had thought kindly enough of her to purchase such a gift, where they had bought it and when. Such information became stories in themselves. We never tired of listening to them even though we knew them by heart. "Oh, I know, I know," as she handled a pair of earrings "Uncle Sam and Aunt Ruby gave them to you, right?" (I thought our country was named after our Uncle Sam for he never left our home after one of his infrequent visits without secreting a one hundred dollar bill into Mom's hand. I also thought Ruby was named for all the red jewelry she wore). With a slight smile and a nod she recounted the trip that she and our dad had taken to visit them in California back in '29. Those were hard times she told us; no money, no jobs, a time when she and my father went in search of employment only to find it a fruitless journey then returning to Montana. We pictured them in their Model-A Ford, camping out and joining hundreds of other people searching in vain for some way to support their families. They were newlyweds. Our father had spent his life on his family's farm; our mother, a one-room schoolteacher, was not allowed to teach after becoming a married woman. After six months of moving from place to place they rented a farm not far from our present home. However, we were more interested in far-away exotic places than our parents' early struggles. Remembering the cold outside our questions were more along the lines of: "Can you really swim in California in the winter? Are they swimming right now? Is the ocean really blue? Can you really pick oranges off the trees in your own backyard?" She patiently answered each question with real life experiences or from information, which she had been given first hand by "someone who knew." The earrings found their original place and she picked up a silver broach fashioned in the shape of a Road Runner. "This is the one your Aunt Clara sent to me before she died." We let a moment linger out of respect before taking turns handling it. "Didn't she marry Uncle George when he returned from the WWII?" Didn't they travel on the train all the way to Arizona for their honeymoon?" "Can Road Runners really outrun a car?" "Have you ever seen one?" "Isn't it hot down there and filled with cactus and can't you drink the cactus juice if you're thirsty and can't you fry eggs on the sidewalk?" "How hot can it get anyway?" Same questions, same answers but the repetition made images dance and fired our desire for more. The bird returned to its "nest" and piece after piece made their debut. Countless gifts from family and friends with a memory attached to each, not one piece had she purchased herself. They all glittered and sparkled until, eventually, one of us would point to the small, delicate diamond ring set in white gold. "Now, you know that's the ring your dad gave to me for our engagement." "How did you meet him?" "You won dancing contests didn't you?" "Didn't he like to sing?" "Why don't you wear it, you still wear your wedding band?" We knew responses here tended to be short but we always tried to elicit more information. If and when new details emerged they helped create a fuller image that we could carry with us, dreaming about having two parents like the ones our friends enjoyed.

The extensive collection represented a great deal of The United States and we would talk of amazing wonders: oceans so blue and huge you couldn't see the opposite shore; a waterfall in New York that was wider than our entire block and a million times higher than the tallest building in Montana; a canyon in Arizona deeper and longer than one could possibly imagine! What would it be like to see those places, meet different people and start building collections of our own? We wiled away the hours and when the last piece was returned to its resting place the lid slowly closed, our flying carpet landed, Mom moved back into her own world and we were left with dreams of our own. Looking out of the frost-patterned windows the "fever" subsided as we talked of where we might like to go, what we wanted to do with our lives. These flights were so customary that it was not until after her death at the age of eighty that I realized their impact.

A few days after her funeral, Mom's jewelry box was placed upon the dining room table. It was Mom's wish that each of us take the pieces we had given her and then divide the rest as we saw fit. Watching another person open the box struck me as an invasion. Adults ourselves, we had taken our own carpet rides and found ourselves flung across the country. We began to build our own memories and collections in addition to expanding hers. Every time we went home, we would ask to look into her jewelry box. It did not matter if we went alone or had a group gathering, the ritual was unchanged and we never tired of the same stories or new ones that had been added after we had left.

I picked up the silver and turquoise ring I had bought her for a birthday she spent in Arizona with the youngest sister. Another story. The second item was a pair of silver earrings with petit-point flowers purchased in Austria. Another story. I left the room to place them in my suitcase and upon returning was struck by the scene. For there, gathered around the table were all of my siblings fingering the pieces as she used to do, choosing which ones they were claiming or reclaiming. As I moved closer to the group I heard an echo of the past: "Oh, remember? This is the bracelet that Aunt Izzy gave her from her trip to Washington D.C.", "Wait, I remember when she got these from each of you boys when you were stationed in Japan", "Remember these....?" Family history remembered, retold, relished.

Then I realized how powerful and valuable that box was, but, more importantly, the enduring spirit of its owner.

Theresa Corbin

The Me I Want to Be

You know what they say about books and their covers. As a woman, I have many chapters, and under my cover I am not always what I seem to others. You wouldn't believe it with just one glance, but I am independent, always intensely imaginative, industrious, and aboriginal. Oh yes, and you may have guessed, I am a Muslim trying to do her best. Wasn't always like that ... used to be a Catholic. The parents said that was best. Never trusted other peoples' "truths"; Something said to search and see for me. Found peace in Islam, found balance, found myself. Gave up everything, lost even more; fought, struggled, was very poor; gained everything, and am excited to see what's in store. You know what they say about books and their looks. To my "own" I am the "other"; a despised stranger in my native land, the dirty south. From my conversion in Louisiana to my life now in Alabama, I have had eggs aimed at my face, curses flung from fearful mouths and middle fingers, mosques lit and burned to the ground. I am sorry some are ignorant and scared, but I am not their enemy, I am not my cover. May I suggest a deeper reading? In the eye of stormy adversity, I know serenity and I yearn for yours.

Marylee MacDonald

The Ugly Duckling, Chinese Babies, and Me

Hans Christian Anderson's story, "The Ugly Duckling," had a deep effect on me when I first heard it read. Andersen was a tall, awkward child who refused to learn a trade. He tried acting and eventually wound up writing stories. The "ugly duckling"—the awkward, teenage Andersen, or perhaps Andersen, the artist and outsider—spoke to me, the small child trying to figure out who I was and where I fit in. My face burned when waitresses stopped their order-taking. Eyebrows pinched, they looked around the triangle of our family. My homely mother, and hard-drinking, longshoreman father were in their fifties and far from the bloom of youth. With bleached blue eyes, they both were blonds. A dark-haired, black-eyed Irish girl, I was an apple with two oranges. From the time I could crawl under the bed and fish out dust bunnies, I knew I was adopted.

Forty-five when she adopted me, my mother, Lorene Pitney Benham, is pictured on the right.

When I see Chinese children adopted by Anglo families, I think of how I coped with never seeing anyone who looked like me. I coped by emotionally shutting down, by standing apart, by extreme self-consciousness about my difference, and ultimately, by rage. There is a subtle process by which a child, yanked out of its natural environment and plopped down in another, attempts to conform and behave and sickeningly (to oneself) be a good girl and *please everyone*. There is a way in which the family looks on a child's natural attributes as alien and threatening. Where did that anger come from? Do you suppose it came from *them*? And what about that sense of humor? That shows disrespect. *Stomp it out.*

I heard about bad tendencies a lot. And it was always the bad tendencies that came from my biological self, the part I couldn't do anything about. Those tendencies could only be corrected by discipline: soap in the mouth, shaming, and time-outs. The usual happy-adoptive-child stuff. When you are adopted, none of the signals—visual or verbal—are familiar to you. Nothing resonates with your DNA. You have landed on Mars and all the communications are in Martian, not in your native tongue.

This adoption thing is sort of the ultimate identity quest, the duckling mocked by siblings until he discovers he's really a swan. Some adoptees are ashamed, some angry, and some refuse to even think about their biological heritage. The latter are appropriately grateful, as they have been coached to be. They are the *good* adoptees. When they visit a doctor, they will even give their biological parents' medical histories on questionnaires. Loyalty is *the* virtue in adoptive families. I wanted to be the good adoptee, but it just wasn't in me.

My own adoption history is pretty dense. I was adopted as an infant and, at thirty-five, searched for my birthparents. Yes, yes, my adoptive parents had passed by then. I didn't have to seek their approval, or I'm not sure I could have gone ahead. As a therapist once told me, I had been "well trained." Kind of like a dog.

My expecting mother, Mary Kathryn Kirkpatrick, age fifteen. I am under the cat.

Part of that training came from the Catholic Church. I had been an obedient teenager until the hormones kicked in. In love with my husband,

also an honor student, I had my first child at sixteen and surrendered him for adoption. Later, I learned how common it was for women adoptees of my generation (I'm sixty-five) to become pregnant and surrender their first-born children, an odd psychodrama that led, in the days before birth control, to the phenomenon of many adoptees becoming birth mothers or birth fathers. Like those who surrendered their first-born children, I tried to "make it right" two years later. Pregnant again, I married the young man I had been in love with. We had four more kids in quick succession. Perhaps,

The first time I met my mother, Mary Kathryn Kirkpatrick. I was thirty-five.

that, too, was fated. My husband died when he was twenty-five. I only wish my oldest son, valedictorian of his university, could have met his father, a Ph.D. from Stanford. Seeing his father's face would have really blown him away. Instead, he spent the Christmas of our reunion up in the attic, exhuming his father's old report cards, trying to imagine the man who provided half of his DNA and brains.

When I saw my mother for the first time, Mary Kathryn Kirkpatrick--a blonde, Betty Grable lookalike--I knew how my oldest son felt. Teeth chattering, muscles twitching, I almost fainted. I found three half-sisters and a half-brother on that side of the family, the first time in my life I'd ever seen anyone who looked like me. My sisters were Phi Beta Kappas, emotional eaters whose weight shot up and down, and verbal about their feelings. Irreverent and sassy, they're powerhouse women who love to help people. I fit right in.

Of my father, Richard Poynton? Dark-haired, with one blue eye and one brown, in his youth he was supposed to have been quite the ladies' man. Very similar to my adoptive father, ironically. Richard worked as a tile-setter and

spent much of his life in jail for kiting checks. He date-raped my mom. She was fifteen. These pieces of information took a while to absorb, but finally settled in.

For many years, I worked as a carpenter, one of the first women in the construction trades. Before I found my father, I had wondered where that aptitude came from, that second brain in the fingers. My sister from that side of the family said, "There could be thousands like you." Maybe. I'd like to think so, because although I am terrible about keeping my checkbook reconciled, I don't think I turned

Marylee Patricia Benham, at age five.

out so bad. At least now, I know how the pieces of nature and nurture fit. The mother who raised me valued education. Because of her, I went to Vassar and Stanford. From my beautiful young mother whose life was disrupted by the trauma of my conception, I inherited my writing ability and yo-yo dieting. Thanks, Mom! But, oddly, when I look in the mirror, my father's face is the one I see. Besides an aptitude for working in a trade, the gift he gave me was his smile.

Stephanie Millett

Whispers of Strangers

It was shaping up to be a typical Monday night. So far, mostly hospital admission reports had routed to me to transcribe. Their subjects consisted of crumpled men and women far past their humane expiration date, most suffering from pneumonia, some with heart failure mixed in—but all suffering. Yes, the night was nothing extraordinary, simply a typical night.

Working from home definitely had its advantages. A load of laundry was only seconds away, and it was nice to get a break from the monotony of sitting at my desk in the corner of my bedroom, my only company the doctors' droning voices hundreds of miles away coming into my room through the invisible web. I had never met the doctors personally or even held a conversation with any of them, but I knew each one's habits intimately; there was Fast Frank, Slurring Stan, and my favorite, Paper Shuffling Paul.

Too often the doctors would multitask, sometimes sneaking dinner in while dictating. The gnawing sound of liquefied food partially muffled through the phone receiver nauseated me. I pictured chunks of turkey, cheese, mayo, and bread taking flight, somehow hurling hundreds of miles toward me. Something never sat quite right in my gut at the thought of Dr. So-and-So dictating grandma's death summary over a turkey club, explaining her demise as the result of aspiration of vomitus while extubation during a standard cholecystectomy or, even worse, chewing his cud during the descriptive discourse of a colonoscopy with polyp removal. Yet it was reality, all of it—the turkey sandwich, colon polyps, grandma's death.

Nurses' laughter would occasionally break through as well, and I found myself faced with the annoyance of obnoxious laughter distorting the doctors' words. Sometimes, I would catch snippets of random conversations in the background: "...wouldn't tell me why..." "...and then she said..." "...they plan on telling him..." These extraneous conversations proved nothing more than a nuisance and of no particular interest to me. Hospital gossip had no bearing on the reality of my desk in the corner of my bedroom.

As I uploaded the report I had just finished transcribing, the next downloaded: An admission history and physical report, but not just any admission report, a transplant admission report. Good news: Someone was getting an organ, a kidney. Bad news: Someone died to donate that kidney— the proverbial balance of hope and loss, a balance of which I was all too acquainted.

As I began the report, it flowed much as the others. But partway through, my fingers stopped, silenced by disbelief. Had I heard the doctor right? Had he just uttered those words? "The donor is a 15-year-old male brain-dead from a self-inflicted gunshot wound."

My blood stilled. My heart slowed. I rewound the dictation and listened again to ensure my ears had not mistaken me. I sat, astonished. The doctor never, never spoke of the donor; never tread on the unspeakable soil of the travesty that lead to this glorious second chance at life for his desperate, deserving patient. Yet, here it was reverberating in my ears: A 15-year-old boy brain-dead from a self-inflicted gunshot wound.

I removed my earbuds. I pushed my chair back. I sat, taking a moment of silence for this boy, this broken boy, and for his mother, his broken mother. Her Universe had violently shifted, torn. All she feared no longer mattered, for the unthinkable had happened. All she accepted as truth now terrified and infuriated her.

I see her reach out for anything to stop her descent into the deep nothingness gaping below her as she sits next to him in the ICU, the smell of antiseptic and urine mingling in her nostrils. She cannot bear to touch him, for this flesh in front of her no longer houses her son but is simply the fleshy, earthy remnant of something more, someone remarkable. A blue hue discolors his lips. She listens to the hum of the ventilator, his precious chest rising and falling in tune to its beat. His feet stick out from the sterile, white sheet, and she notices his toenails need trimmed. His long hair drapes over his eyes, but she cannot bear to wisp it back. Yes, his long hair baffled the medics, deceiving them to believe he is a girl—but alas, he is a boy, her boy.

The day wears on, and nurses, doctors, and case workers glide in and out, some talking to her or holding her hand and others just moving around her son, adjusting a tube or injecting a med. She looks out the window. She rages. How can the world possibly continue, oblivious to the enormous rent now fissuring its surface? She hates all she sees. She hates the woman clinging to her newborn wrapped in a blanket of powder blue. She hates the teenage boy in the red baseball cap with a fresh cast on his arm. She hates the young woman in canary yellow scrubs scurrying to her car. She despises them all.

In the midst of her confusion and disbelief, this woman makes a decision: The decision to donate her son's organs.

I wept.

I wept for this faceless, nameless woman, for her anguish, for her utter loss. I wept for the graduation she would never attend, the daughter-in-law she would never know, the grandchildren she would never embrace. I wept for the guilt and emptiness that lay ahead in her path. I felt this woman like few others could, for I myself had sat next to my own son in the ICU, my boy with the long hair, those same words echoing in my mind: "I know there is never an appropriate time for this question, but have you considered donating your son's organs?"

This woman, who neither knew of my existence nor of my tears now freely flowing for her, this woman and I shared an unearthly connection. Our sons had both left this world on their own terms, in their fear and fierceness. We had both wrestled this horror and both came to the same conclusion: I must find meaning in this senselessness. I must grasp this opportunity for my son's tragedy to uplift the tiniest corner of the world, even while my tiny corner splinters.

After some time, sitting at my desk in the corner of my bedroom, I wiped my tears. Gathering my pain, I gingerly poured it back into its jar, capped it tightly, and gently placed it on the highest shelf of my heart. However, tonight, this familiar ritual included placing this woman's memory on the shelf next to my jar.

My fingers once again found the keyboard, and I finished typing the report.

I still frequently visit this woman, up on my heart-shelf. I find myself whispering to her, whispering fragmented, broken thoughts I can confide in no one else, and for a moment, I find relief.

Francis DiClemente

One More Day
Christmas Day, mid-1990s

As we drove along Route 365 westbound, headed for the New York State Thruway and Syracuse's Hancock Airport, nature's tapestry unfolded outside the windows of the Chevy Blazer. The rolling hills of Oneida County stretched out to meet a blue-gray layer of sky, and gaunt and naked tree branches gave way to thick pine trees, which accepted the brunt of the early winter storm. Fat wet snowflakes slapped against the windshield and perished, while outside, they lost their individuality as they formed a thin white icing on the sloping fields and surrounding farmland. But some blades of grass still strained to break through the snow, and when they triumphed, looked like Mom's squiggly, Pig-Pen fibers of hair, as chemotherapy had claimed most of her black hair, dyed to the roots prior to her illness.

She concealed her bald head with a red felt hat adorned with a black velvet band, which if you can imagine, appeared like the midsection of a skinny Santa Claus. A brush stroke of rouge on both cheeks and a dab of lipstick spruced up Mom's face, but could not conceal the snide grin of lung cancer underneath. Her eyes seemed like black pinholes emanating a waning light, and she made no apology for her sour disposition. It was clear she did not approve of my sister Lisa and me traveling home to Toledo, Ohio on Christmas Day.

"What would one more day hurt?" she had asked before we left the house in nearby Rome. When we rattled off a list of obligations, she countered with, "Just forget I asked. It's obvious it means nothing to either of you." She tried to lace her words with vitriol, but her voice sounded wounded instead.

It seemed ironic that Mom was so upset about us leaving on Christmas because our childhood experience indicated she had no fondness for holidays. My sister and I could not count the number of times our mother had spoiled holidays, birthdays and special occasions throughout the years. Before my parents divorced in the 1980s, my mother loathed going to my father's parents' house for any family gathering. Sometimes she would remain in her room, sleeping, crying or feigning sickness, and refusing to get in the car and go. It became our job to make up excuses when we went to our grandparents without her; usually, we just said, "Mom's not feeling very well today." Of course, this became an overused expression.

I never understood why she behaved like this, but I knew it wasn't normal. I wondered if my mother's problems stemmed from depression, serious emotional troubles or whether they just came down to the fact she was miserable living with my father and lashed out in response to the unhappy conditions of her married life. However, my mother's behavior did not change after she remarried in the early 1990s. I remember one Christmas Eve or New Year's Eve she did not want to have any people over the house to celebrate. Well we decided to hold a party without her because my stepfather had already invited the guests; and so, in customary form, my mother stayed up in her room while we ate dinner downstairs with family and friends, and I surmised the laughter rising from the dining room likely reached her ears through the heat vent in her bedroom. And our actions resulted in a silent treatment from my mother in the days following the party.

* * * * *

Bill, my stepfather, kept the Blazer steady on the road while Mom's aspect—as captured in the right side view mirror—remained like an ice sculpture. Meanwhile, I picked up the plastic grocery bag in the backseat and took a quick inventory of the booty accompanying us to the Midwest. Mom had packed a loaf of B&L Italian bread and some other goodies—which I cannot recall exactly, but likely included pepperoni, salami or provolone cheese, along with some of her homemade pizzelles and Italian Christmas cookies.

But the delicacies of Rome, New York failed to excite me because I knew they came paired with my mother's melancholy. Don't get me wrong, our commitments were in no way fabricated. We explained long before we flew home that our stay was limited. As a corporate attorney for Toledo Edison, Lisa was due to resume her legal work in the morning, on December 26th, and I had to get back to the newsroom of Newsradio 1370 WSPD, where I worked as an assignment editor and producer.

Exit 36 off the New York State Thruway took us closer to our destination. Looking out the window, I spotted flashing red lights above the horizon and heard the distant roar of commercial jet engines. Grapefruit-colored street lights lined the roadway leading to the airport, which now crept into sight. There was nothing else to think about except how to say goodbye without hurting my mother even more. The task appeared futile and time slipped away beyond the point of recovery.

We pulled over to the curb in front of the USAir terminal. Bill turned off the radio and the sound of the heater resonated inside the cramped space, but my mother's silence felt like an indictment. Bill popped the back hatch as Lisa and I scurried outside the driver's side door; in doing so, we allowed Mom to remain in her seat. We also hurried to avoid being slapped with a ticket by a watchful Syracuse traffic cop. We quickly handed off our bags to the USAir porters stationed curbside and then turned to say goodbye to Mom.

"You kids be careful," Bill barked out in a frosty breath. Lisa reached up to kiss him while I patted him ardently on his back.

Mom, on the other hand, was intent on forcing a dramatic finale. She remained in the car with the window cracked halfway as she puffed on a Salem Light cigarette. I stepped toward the car with my sister following close behind.

"You better hurry or you'll miss your flight," Mom said with her eyes focused on the side view mirror. A spire of smoke rose from the tips of her thin fingers before being snatched away by a gust of wind.

"Mom, you know we don't mean to do this," I said. When she failed to speak or even glance at me, I circled the front end of the Blazer until I was directly within her eye-line. I recall either my sister or myself saying something like, "We'll be back again soon Mom," to which my mother responded, "Why bother?"

Bill then attempted to intercede on our behalf. "Carm, please…"

"Enough," she said, jamming her fist into the dashboard, "just let them go."

I reached my head inside the window and kissed my mother. Black spots shaped like crescents stood out under her eyes, but no tears glided along the surface of her pallid cheeks. She maintained a visual stalemate by refusing to look at me, and hence, I wished to lop off—in one swift machete slice—the petty preoccupations that lurked in the land of tomorrow. "If you really want us to stay, we will," I said. I admit the words were intended solely to mollify Mom; but after saying them to her face, I was suddenly overcome by an impulse to carry through on this spontaneous plan.

My sister, however, was not on board with the effort and shot me a glare. Mom opened the car door, shifted around in her seat and settled her narrow frame on the curb. Then she moved forward with a surge of strength, wrapped her arms around me and squeezed. She did the same to my sister, and as they hugged, Mom's hat tipped up, revealing her bald head.

"I know you can't stay," she said with a sigh. She clasped my hands and added, "Please go. I'll feel exactly the same way tomorrow."

"No you won't," I said.

"Yes I will. And the same goes for the day after that."

"Do you mean it?" I asked.

She nodded, and like an actor's cue, I resumed the task of checking the bags. I tipped the baggage man extra for the delay. And then, after the absolute final goodbyes were exchanged, my sister and I slipped past the automatic doors and into the USAir terminal. But as we moved along the slick and shiny floor inside, I looked over my shoulder and snagged one last peek of my mom, who remained standing at the curb in front of her opened passenger door. She waved as if she had expected me to turn around, waiting to quash any lingering indecisiveness on my part.

And her accompanying smile made leaving that much easier.

* * * * *

The plane was delayed in Pittsburgh for over forty minutes and we hit some turbulence en route to Toledo. My right shoulder ached from the coarse nylon strap of my duffel bag, my face felt flushed and warm and I could not muster the energy to unpack my suitcase and wash the dirty clothes.

I opened Mom's bag and made a provolone cheese sandwich with the fresh Italian bread. I envisioned Mom neatly packing the grocery bag with items my sister and I would enjoy once we arrived home. And I remembered dipping that same Italian bread from B&L into steaming bowls of my mother's homemade lentil soup or pasta fagioli on cold winter evenings.

And I forced my mind not to forget my mother's image or dismiss her behavior at the airport because it was painful to contemplate what could happen down the road. I wondered if she would still be around the following year. And that gnawing fear left me feeling guilty. The previous Christmas I had not given it a second thought before heading home after the holidays, and deadline pressures and daily commitments meant work would probably always take precedence over my family.

The question now, though, was not, "had cancer changed things?" Instead, I asked myself while munching on the sandwich, "Why did I need a disease to come into our lives in order to fully appreciate my mother?"

I think it was because for so long, my sister and I had tolerated our mother—enduring her mood swings, incessant smoking and ruined holidays. We still loved her and needed her, but it was easier to love Mom from afar, out of her range.

Yet those were our issues. I had to look inside myself and beyond the troubles of the past and see the situation from my mother's perspective—from the vantage point of someone suffering from cancer and unsure of what the future would bring. Of course she would be upset about her children leaving her on Christmas Day. She just wasn't ready to let us go; like any mother, she wanted more time with her kids. And for her, time could not be relied on. It could only be measured by one more day.

128

Marilyn June Janson

Letters to Linny

While growing up, I can't recall having many conversations with my Dad. For years we drifted through our lives like strangers on a train.

From the day after school ended in June until the day before classes began again in September, my parents sent me to an overnight camp in Logan Canyon, Utah. I spent ten summers away from home.

Sad, lonely, and scared, I didn't make friends easily. Because this was long before the advent of computers and e-mail, Kee-Wah campers were required to write home on stamped self-addressed postcards provided by our parents. Campers were not permitted to make "distress" phone calls to anyone on the outside.

> June 30
> Dear Mom,
> Help! I miss you. I want to go home.
> Love,
> Linny

I was surprised when it was Dad, not Mom, who responded. On unlined, letter-sized, white paper, he wrote:

> July 8
> Dear Linny,
> I miss you too, but you must not be a quitter. Have fun playing baseball and tennis. Make new friends. Did you have fun on July 4th?
> Love,
> Dad

As if it were the title of a book, I began to write the word "Troubles" at the top of every postcard. My sister Barbara, five years older than I, was a camper in the teen-age division. On Sundays we were supposed to spend time together. Instead, I sat alone on a bench while Barbara and her boyfriend flirted with each other. Feeling abandoned while other siblings hung out together, I wrote to my Dad.

> July 15
> Troubles
> Dear Dad,
> I am very sad. Barbara does not want to be with me on Sundays.
> Love,
> Linny.

July 22
Dear Linny,
You must learn to be a big girl. Your sister has her own friends. What is your favorite sport at camp?
Love,
Dad

July 28
Troubles
Dear Dad,
I'm last to get picked for baseball. I painted a rock and drew a picture.
Love,
Linny

August 5
Dear Linny,
Your sister writes that she is having so much fun. Try to be like her. Instead of drawing and painting, practice playing tennis and baseball and then you then you will get good at them like Barbara.
Love,
Dad

On their birthday, my popular bunkmates, the Blonkowitz twins, gave me horseback riding lessons. I fell in love with the horses. Finally, I had found something that I couldn't fail at. The kind, handsome, muscular animals seemed to accept me despite my low tennis ranking.

August 12
Troubles
Dear Dad,
I want to ride the horses! Please, please call the camp and tell them to let me ride. I'll try so very hard to be good at everything else. I'll make some friends.
Love,
Linny

August 19
Dear Linny,
Your Mom is afraid that you'll get hurt. Who is your best friend at camp?
Love,
Dad

When I read the letter, I cried. Why couldn't they ever let me have anything that I wanted?

On Parents' Day, Mom and Dad came to the stables and watched me ride. Proudly, I sat upon that quarter horse and held the reins. I felt like Caroline Kennedy, America's royalty. "Let's go, boy," I told the horse. We trotted around the corral. When they saw me ride, Mom and Dad finally gave me their permission to continue with it.

At last, I had something just for me. With a guide and some other campers, I rode into the mountains. I breathed in the Christmassy scent of Bristlecone Pine and listened to the horses' hooves hitting the ground as we carefully passed over streams, rocks, and fallen branches. I acquired confidence with the newfound mastery I felt.

The letters we exchanged were in essence the first time I remember having a "conversation" with my Dad. During my first camp experience, and for the following summers, we continued to write. I learned to find hope and happiness despite my loneliness and sadness. At age 16, my camp days were over. We never wrote to each other again.

Many years after Mom died, Dad passed away. While cleaning out my parents' bedroom, I found those postcards and letters in a dresser drawer, tucked under his colorful madras handkerchiefs.

Janet Amalia Weinberg

Just Happening

People think differently in India, or so it seemed as I stood on the banks of the Ganges, surrounded by sixty million Hindu pilgrims who had come to the river to bathe. *I* thought the water was polluted and could make me sick— I'd seen garbage, excrement, and three dead bodies in it. *They* thought it was holy and could cleanse them of sin.

Such gatherings, called *Kumbha Melas*, occur periodically at various sacred bathing sites in India, but this was a *Maha Kumbha Mela*, a particularly auspicious event that happens once every hundred and forty four years. According to legend, the universal forces for good are so concentrated at this time that simply attending the *Mela* can purify many lifetimes. I was at a change point in life and had come, not to dip in the Ganges, but to immerse myself in this positive consensus reality.

It was the largest pilgrimage on the planet and a temporary city of perhaps a million army tents had been erected for the month-long happening. I was camped just outside the *Mela* grounds in an enclave of 400 other Westerners from the States.

One day, a group of us from my camp got a ride to hear the Dalai Lama speak. A crowd of tens of thousands was expected so we left early. As our car entered the *Mela*, we were swept into a sensory tsunami. People were everywhere--riding rickshaws and Land Rovers, camels and donkeys, walking, standing, cooking, praying, waiting, sleeping. Groups from distant villages sat along the dusty roads. Vendors sold cabbages, peanuts, onions, potatoes, and eggplants. Women, drying freshly washed saris in the wind, unfurled eighteen-foot banners of color. *Sadhus*–holy men with flowing beards and penetrating eyes--hiked to and from the Ganges. Cows roamed. Competing public address systems blared chants and prayers. Smoke from a million dung cooking fires clogged the air and the smell of incense, sandalwood and curry sweetened it.

The sixty square mile tent-city was divided into sectors. There were no street signs, but temples and religious groups had their own encampments with identifying gateways. We were in such sensory overload that we probably had passed the same gateways over and over before we noticed our driver was taking us in circles.

Ordinarily I would have thought: "We're lost, we might miss the Dalai Lama, it's all the driver's fault...." But I didn't think what was happening was bad or wrong. In fact, I didn't think about it at all; it was just happening.

As the driver wandered, I marveled at the sights. I had only explored the *Mela* on foot; seeing it by car was an unexpected bonus. Along the way, we met another lost car, packed with Westerners from our camp. While the drivers conferred, we exchanged stares with a *sadhu* – he with his orange *dhoti*, glazed red eyes and Vishnu trident, we with our sun hats, dark glasses and sneakers. Eventually, with reassuring nods, the drivers resumed their quest.

When we finally reached our destination, we found a crowd churning with rumors that the Dalai Lama would not appear. Again, I could have gotten disappointed, but my new and strange state of accepting and going with the flow was still with me.

Suddenly a vehicle shot out of the compound. Someone yelled, "There goes the Dalai Lama!" and our vehicles took off in hot pursuit. Now it seemed we were lucky to have gotten lost. Otherwise, our drivers would have dropped us off earlier and we, like all those people we left behind, would have had no transportation.

The chase ended at a small tent. There were eleven of us now, five from my car and six, including a two-man camera crew, from the other. We removed our shoes and entered the tent. Menacing guards armed with uzi's scrutinized us but let us pass. Inside, the Dalai Lama was kneeling in prayer before an altar. Behind him, about fifty Indians, mostly *sadhu's* in traditional orange and ochre robes, sat cross-legged on mats. Our two carloads clustered at the rear of the tent.

After a few moments, His Holiness, speaking Tibetan, began addressing the gathering through a Hindi translator. People asked questions he must have heard countless times, but he gave each person his full attention and responded with genuine caring. When he finished talking with the Indians, he smiled and called to us in English, "Come on up!"

We closed in around him, astounded by our good fortune. Instead of being part of a crowd of thousands, we had been practically granted a private audience. He signed autographs, laughed, spoke of world peace, and expressed his pleasure at seeing Westerners at the *Mela*. His radiant delight captivated us all.

When the Dalai Lama rose to leave, a dozen Tibetans immediately formed a human fence along both sides of his path to the exit. He passed through, like a whoosh of joy, stopping to give one *sadhu's* beard a playful tug and pat another's cheek before he left.

When I exited the tent, my companions were waiting outside. Our car was not. The second carload, including the camera crew, was gone as well. We were all hot and tired and ready to return to our camp. There was just one hitch: we didn't know where it was.

We gathered at the side of the road to look for a taxi, a rickshaw, a pony cart – anything that could take us back. For as far as we could see, the dusty road was flanked by tents and teeming with people, but there were no vehicles. None. We tried to get directions, but those we asked either didn't understand English or had never heard of our camp. Even if we had known which way to go, two members of our group were somewhat handicapped and couldn't walk very far.

Normally, I would have been alarmed and anxious. But as before, I didn't judge what was happening or think anything about it; it was just happening. I don't know if being at the *Mela* purified lifetimes, but it sure was purifying my habit of evaluating and interpreting every experience.

We sat on some boxes, conveniently piled by the side of the road, watched the crowd, and waited. Five minutes passed . . . ten . . . fifteen. . . . Suddenly, a black sedan appeared! Before any of us could wave to it, the car screeched to a halt in front of us.

The door flung open and out stepped the leader of the group I was staying with. The leader! He had come to meet the Dalai Lama and found us instead. When we informed him that His Holiness had left, he got back into his car and sped away—but not before he'd whipped out a cell phone and called for a car to pick us up.

We were giddy. How amazing! How perfect! We could never have hoped for or imagined such a rescue. As we waited for the car to arrive, someone joked, "Now all we need is a parade." As if by magic, a procession complete with music, painted elephants, camels, and row after row of marchers appeared.

That's how it was at the *Mela*. Ordinary thinking, full of expectations and judgments, seemed to fall away and every disrupted plan became an adventure.

Now, back in my regular life, I have plenty of opportunity to get upset when things don't go "right." Car batteries die, keys get lost, people disappoint me, I disappoint myself—the possibilities are endless. But that also means I have plenty of opportunity to remember the *Mela* and to see what's happening as just what's happening.

Terry Meyer Stone

If I Were More Feminine

If I were more feminine, I would wear long flowery dresses and matching underwear that I'd purchased at Victoria's Secret or maybe Vie En Rose instead of the Costco special of three for the price of one. I'd have a bra that fit and pushed me up pertly instead of my mother's old-new one-- given to me when she shrunk at eighty-three-- that now hangs on my over-padded middle-aged voluptuous bosom, like the prow of the ship leading me into each room.

If I were more feminine,

If I were more feminine,

If I were more feminine, I wouldn't curse so much, or burp or fart. My feet wouldn't be size 10. I wouldn't sneeze like I was calling in a spell, bringing down all the forces of nature, swirled and twirled into gigantic momentum and screamed with semi joy and slight pain and total irreverence into my sleeve-- or straight into the air if no one was watching.

If I were more feminine, I would dance with rhythm gently, sinuously, seductively instead of like a primal Ubangi native in his first hunting rites, blood thirsty and primitive, arms jerking to the potion and spells of the local witchdoctor, mirroring ecstasy and throes of fear. If I were more feminine, I'd whisper softly 'pardon me', instead of 'what' and 'huh', and 'what the fuck' and would laugh with a gentle tinkle like the wind chimes outside my window instead of braying like a donkey.

If I were more feminine, I would cook cookies and bake cakes and have a clean kitchen and do laundry and have a floor that you could eat off. I would have matching plates and cups and cool napkins and kitchen cutlery that looked like I was rich. If I were more feminine my walls would be painted in a pleasing palate and the pictures dusted and I'd be more polite to strangers, because now they would be allowed in my no- longer- messy house.

If I were more feminine,

If I were more feminine,

If I were more feminine, men would follow me down the aisles of home depot because they would smell something on me, the aroma of sex or girl or magic or pheromone that some women drop behind them. If I were more feminine I would have welcomed breast feeding and made my own baby food and learned how to sew. I wouldn't have been kicked out of home economics with the only F that I was ever to get in my entire academic history, the pain of which was only assuaged by winning the Black Diamond Cowboy bar title for fastest beer chugging, having mastered that in only 2.2 seconds. I wouldn't have loved the thrill of competition and the fierce joy of my pounding legs running and my pounding fists fighting when I was twelve, I would have phoned boys and wrote them yearning, mooning notes and worn lipstick instead.

If I were more feminine I wouldn't have crone hairs sprouting from my chin, or the fine long down of moustache and cheek that I catch in the reflection of my rearview mirror while driving —when of course no tweezers are ever in sight and I forget by the time I get home. If I were more feminine, I wouldn't sweat like a farmer and have discolored rings beneath my armpits; I would be dewy and glow. If I were more feminine I wouldn't ever have to think about sweat or beer or if my fantasy hockey team was playing up to par. I would spend more time waxing my legs, and wear perfume. I would have gone to tea parties, and baby showers and PTA meetings, instead of hiding at home in my pajamas reading books. I wouldn't long for sex, rough and sweaty and crazy, even though I undress in the closet and pretend I'm asleep at night. I wouldn't talk back or rebel against rules, I wouldn't argue with my husband's point of view and I would be kinder to my children than I am to my dogs. My children would be more perfect, more polished and polite and never misbehave or get dirty or drunk and arrested.

I would give more, love more, be loved more, be less hairy, be sweeter, be quieter, be gentler, be nicer, oh and above all I'd be nicer.

If I were more feminine,

If I were more feminine,

If I were more feminine.

We

Charlotte Jones

Simple Pleasures

Once upon a time
it was scaling a rope
to the very top
in gym class,
seeing the dried
corsages of
distant proms displayed
on my memory board,
strumming a Cmaj7
and knowing the
guitar was in tune.

Later,
it was celebrating the
completion of a project,
marveling at the
colorful life
on a coral reef,
finding some good sex.

Now
it is knowing
my heart is shared
with another,
hearing his quiet
breathing in our bed,
feeling the sun
on our backs
on a cool autumn day,
sharing those rare moments
when there is nothing
we have to do.

Christine Minter

The Child I Wanted, But Was Afraid to Have

Miracles do happen. I am thinking today about our daughter and I don't know what I would do without her. She thinks I am great, beautiful and smart. The feeling is mutual. She is nine and a half years old now. I know miracles happen because we recently lost our second child months before it was to be born.

Do you know what it's like to become handicapped? The stares you get and the insensitive statements that some well-meaning stranger makes that make you cringe inside, but instead you smile? Friends who don't want you around anymore? And you go on and pretend it doesn't matter – until soon it really doesn't matter.

How would it be to bring a child into the world knowing that they need to be able to look up to their parents? How can you instill pride in your child when each day you have to psyche yourself up to face the world? Would I have the courage, strength, and fortitude to instill in our child what she needed to make it in the world? These are the questions that terrified me when I was told I was pregnant.

Months passed, the mornings were the most difficult. I often had heartburn and frequently could not sleep. Since I had to stop working, I decided to take a class at night to occupy my time. It was good therapy for me because I was constantly worried about the baby since I wasn't able to walk or exercise properly due to the paralysis in my legs. My husband was very concerned, but comforted me. My parents were frightened as they remembered how difficult it was for me to fight back to be as mobile and independent as possible after becoming paralyzed.

My family gave me a surprise baby shower, and we began collecting everything we could think of. We even tried to plan ahead and bought things that would help me when I was alone taking care of the baby. When people asked what we wanted, we replied, "A healthy baby."

During my December check up, my doctor described what would take place during the delivery the following month. He explained that specialists would assist him in the delivery because of the severe spasms in my legs. This check up went well, so he told us which hospital I would be admitted to for the scheduled January 14th Cesarean procedure.

My thoughts were occupied with preparations for Christmas. Shopping, wrapping gifts, and putting up the tree took on a different level of excitement for us. On December 23rd, my water broke. After speaking to the doctor, we were relieved as he answered questions and felt no harm would be done since I wasn't able to move around and confined to a wheelchair. However, throughout the night, this had continued and by 9am on December 24th,

Dr. Hendrix instructed us to get to the hospital. In all the excitement, my husband drove to the wrong hospital and the nurses there had to direct us to Georgia Baptist Hospital, where Dr. Hendrix was waiting.

Once we arrived, he examined me and said that the baby was on its way. I was given some shot and in my fuzziness, was introduced to the specialists who would help with the delivery. That was the last thing I remembered before awaking at about 2pm to William and other family members around the bed smiling. They announced that we had a little girl. Fear immediately crept into my thoughts: Is she healthy? Can she move her legs?

As if reading my thoughts, William replied, "She is healthy, beautiful." She was called a miracle because she was born without a cesarean. Even Dr. Hendrix couldn't believe that she was delivered normally.

Today, nine and a half years later, I still think of Valerie as a miracle. William and I talk about her constantly. Though we lost our second child, and the questions I asked myself almost ten years ago seem senseless, I am a proud handicapped wife and mother.

April C. Thornton

Come on Daddy

On a day that started out the same as the many that came before it, I placed my one-year-old daughter into her car seat and made sure it was secure. After checking to see that my other children were buckled, I turned to my father and said, "Come on daddy lets go to the store." The words reverberated in my mind's ear. Come on daddy, Come on daddy, Come on daddy... As I started the car intending to travel on one path, my mind began to take another journey.

On the high definition screen of my mind I flashed back to various times when I have uttered the words, "Come on daddy." William Lee Thornton Jr., welcomed me into this world at the age of sixty-five, after retiring from thirty years of service as a letter carrier for the United States Postal Service. At a time in his life when most men his age were ready to sit back and relax. Instead, he had me.

As my mind traveled through time I remembered very vividly a younger me, plaits flapping up and down as I ran anxiously through the park trying to make my way to the play area. There he was just a few steps behind keeping a close eye on me as I shouted, "Come on daddy!" I can recall the times at Audubon Park where I ran up the sides of the steep dirt mound and he climbed to the top right behind me to show me how to position myself on my cardboard box before sliding down.

I flashed from scene to scene as though watching a marathon of sitcoms on television. In one scene I saw myself laughing as I skated in City Park, an energetic child seeing no need for him to stop and catch his breath, as I shouted, "Come on daddy!" In another scene I'm running from aisle to aisle putting toys in the basket unaware of the meaning of the expression that occupied his face, or the twitch in his eye. Placing more items in the basket I shouted, "Come on daddy!" One of my favorites was one where I was splashing in the water as this seventy-four year old man took a warm up lap before teaching me how to swim; and again I shouted, "Come on daddy!" Whether it was stopping at a fair we happened to see on the way home, or taking me to the upper deck of the ferry as we sailed across the Mississippi River, pushing his fear of heights aside as he was just a step behind me. Sometimes I called out, "Come on daddy" just because. And, much like the sun rising and setting, without fail, he was there.

Now life has reversed. There have been times when I have called and didn't get an answer only to arrive at his home and discover the phone receiver in the wrong position. Now I call to remind him of a doctor's appointment, or to tell him I have finished his laundry, or remind him to take his medicine, or that I'm bringing over a hot meal before I go to work. It's now my honor to be to him all that he has been to me, always there.

I smile at the road ahead. Putting the car into park, and gathering my children it's with joy that I now say, "Come on daddy, let's get your groceries."

Hal O'Leary

My Son Sean

My Son Sean

I guess when my son Sean was four or five,
I thought just like all dads, here was a kid
Who probably not only would survive,
But be the best at anything he did.

One day I had to undertake a chore
For which I had no taste, and Sean my son
Was playing there beside me on the floor,
A boy, that for an equal, there was none.

The chore I undertook had not gone well,
And so, I asked son Sean to fetch for me
A tool I sorely needed. What the hell,
He'd nothing else to do, his time was free.

"Not now." He said, "I'm busy, can't you see?"
"Good God" I said, "You're busy doing what?
Pray tell me, let me know what that could be?"
He shamed me with the answer that I got.
For what he had to say was oh so true,
"But Dad, there's so much playing I must do."

My Son Sean
(A Regrettable Sequel)

All fathers love their sons a lot.
I'm no exception. No I'm not.
And when he was a little tot,
My good son Sean, or so I thought,
Would be of ties, a real ascot.
I beamed with all the joy he brought,
For he was everything I'd sought
To be the genius I was not.
Although in math he wasn't hot,
He showed that language was his slot.
At six, he read of Camelot,
And of his hero Lancelot.

So as reward for this I bought
A beagle pup for his mascot,
And he should name him, should he not?
I told him just to take a shot.
I knew it as I watched him squat
And knowing that his mind was fraught
With names like Good Sir Lancelot,
For the exotic he would opt.
I waited wondering just what.

But then I trembled, quite distraught,
When looking up, the little snot
Said, *Dad, I know, I'll call him…SPOT.*

My Son Sean
(A welcome sequel)

Well many years have passed, and if I might,
There is another sequel I could cite
As evidence that first thoughts may be right.
For my son Sean, and much to my delight,
Stands tall, his genius now has come to light.
The promise we foresaw has taken flight.

And Dad recalling how this little sprite
He named for Sean O'Casey to excite
The muse he knew would make a future bright
Stands equally as tall. as is his right.
Though standing in the shadows out of sight,
He beams with pride that takes him to the height,
And to himself, it's thought he might recite,
That's my son Sean. He's now a fine playwright.

Cathy Crenshaw Doheny

The Alien Between Us

An alien lives in my chest. He is pretty unobtrusive, just a bump about the size of a stack of quarters implanted subcutaneously. A special instrument, known as a Huber needle, is used to interact with him. This needle has a hole on the side, rather than the tip, which enables an easier entrance into the septum. Once the needle is inserted into my alien, also known as a port-a-cath or port for short, he is given a good bath of saline, followed by a shower of Heparin to clear out any blood clots.

The purpose of the port is to transport medicines into my bloodstream by way of a major vein. The long wormy looking part, called a catheter, is threaded into my vein. The medicine goes through the catheter and straight to my heart, where it is promptly sent out into my bloodstream. My medicine is actually a blood product, known as intravenous immunoglobulin or IVIG. It is comprised of the antibody portion of the blood from a multitude of donors. These normal antibodies race through my body to neutralize my native ones.

My own antibodies seem to be having some sort of identity crisis. They attack parts of me - parts I actually need to function. They most like to attack the myelin sheath, which insulates my peripheral nerves. They eat away this fatty insulation, causing some pretty significant problems, creating what is known as Chronic Inflammatory Demyelinating Polyneuropathy (CIDP), a neurological autoimmune disease. When my CIDP is in full swing, I experience nerve pain, muscle cramps and weakness in my arms and legs, and just plain exhaustion; all because of some mixed up antibodies!

Did I happen to mention that these mutants also enjoy attacking my ovaries in their spare time? Painful arms, cramping legs, complete exhaustion, AND infertility; all caused by this bizarre identity crisis. It seems to me they could have just pooled their resources and gotten a Porsche instead. Shouldn't my cells have at least as much sense as the average middle-aged man?

When my alien first came to live with me, I was a skinny 30-year old, which made his debut a little more noticeable underneath my tight skin. To make matters even worse, I had an unsightly scar of several inches right above him, where the skin was cut for insertion. I soon became Rapunzel, attempting to disguise my visitor. I wore high collars even in the summer, always conscious of what others might think of the alien and what it meant to have him there. I didn't want their curiosity, pity, or disgust. I just wanted to be a young, vibrant woman.

Most of all, I wanted to appear that way to my handsome husband, who moonlighted as a control-freak. I worried that he would no longer find me attractive, now that the alien protruded from my chest. He had not bargained to have a science experiment for a wife. Despite his reassurances, I could not trust that the attraction would continue. I deeply suspected that he had married me for me for my appearance, rather than my many other attributes.

A month later, I discovered that I should never have been so concerned about the effect of my alien inhabitant. I had just driven myself home from a daylong IVIG infusion. My temperature was 101 degrees, and I was experiencing the usual flu-like side effects. My husband was nowhere to be found, an increasingly frequent phenomenon that I found to be particularly unnerving. So in my feverish state, I decided to do a bit of harmless snooping. Notes from his latest novel-in-progress were sitting exposed on his desk, a testament to how trusting and naïve my husband had always known me to be. There it was in his own handwriting: lewd scenes from his affair with a fellow professor. He even provided a chart that compared me to his mistress. He had impressively done his research for this project. I knew enough about my husband's writing to know that he wrote about his own life and hid it behind a "fiction" label. So, there was no question in my mind as to the veracity of his newest material.

The irony of the situation lies in the fact that my husband started his affair nine months prior to my discovery, long before my alien's appearance. True, the affair did commence around the time of my diagnosis of CIDP. I suppose he already sensed what was coming: unattractive things like infusions, surgeries, disabilities, and even an alien invasion. Of course, he would vehemently deny the significance of the timing, citing simply a coincidence. "A mistake in judgment," he had said. Mistake or not, I knew that his judgment would always be flawed. In a relationship, when trust is gone, little else remains worth sticking around for. So, my alien and I packed up and hobbled out the door and out of that marriage.

I had been married for only three years, suffered from a rare chronic illness, carried around an ugly alien in my chest, and now found myself once again single. Having learned too much from my failed marriage, I had very specific ideas about what my qualifications for a mate would be. I was sick of hiding being sick. On first dates, I would cut right to the chase, would spill the whole story to the man across the table from me - divorced, first husband cheated on me, living with my parents now, only working part-time, potentially disabling illness, and oh, did I mention.... I also have an alien living in my chest! If the recipient of that news didn't go running from the restaurant, I knew that I may have found someone worth getting to know.

I have to say, I saw more male backs than faces during the first few months. That is, until I met Kevin. He found my profile on a popular Internet dating site, and was already smitten by the time we talked on the phone. He was so kind; his goodness made me wish my every breath could be consumed with our exchanged words. He told me that it didn't matter where we went on a date; he would be content to sit in a dark closet and just talk to me all night. After that conversation, I told my mother I was going to marry this man.

On our first date, I confided in Kevin my whole story, including the alien who would always be accompanying me. Much to my surprise, his eyes didn't look for the nearest exit. He replied that he was sorry that I had to endure such a horrible illness and that it could never affect the way he felt about me. He explained that I would always be me; the illness could never change that. That was all he cared about - so simple. He just wanted me, for the me who lived in my eyes and laugh and tears. The following week he sat by my side, as IVIG flowed into my alien.

"That doesn't sound like something you should do alone," he had said on that first night.

I told Kevin about my ugly divorce. He said he wanted to send my first husband a fruit basket for being such an idiot to have let me go, so he could now have the pleasure of my presence. We claimed our first kiss that night in front of a fireplace at a quaint coffee house. I felt engulfed in this giant of a man, who reminded me of a medieval warrior. At the late night end of the date, he asked simply, "What do I have to do to get to see you tomorrow?" The heart that neighbors my alien, sighed happily, relieved to have found its refuge from the disappointment of living. Amidst the celebration of sighs, Kevin continued to ask that same question every night until the day we married six months later.

Two and a half years following that glorious day, Kevin had the misfortune of his own alien invasion. At just thirty-five years of age, he was shockingly diagnosed with a rare cancer and needed a port to help him through intravenous chemotherapy. He joked that some couples get matching rings to show their devotion, but we always carried our love beyond expectations. Our matching ports and corresponding scars represent our deep understanding of the other's adversities. More costly than the most expensive diamond ring, that understanding binds our marriage through even the most grotesque alien invasion.

Nancy Nicol

Too Late Daughter

I remember the day my Mother buys the heavenly blue suit. "Do I look French," she asks, "wearing red kid shoes?" After cataract surgery, she is having a love affair with color. Sapphire, of course, a shade to match her new eyes, and purple, mauve, violet. She enjoys the latest styles with short skirts that Dad calls 'too youthful on you, Babe.'

I remember a strong fragrance of Este Lauder on Mom's clothes when she dies two months later. It has soaked into collars of blouses, jackets, even that turquoise bathrobe she wore once in a while. Along with heavenly blue for burial, I choose a lace half-slip, matching bra, nylons, and the red shoes. I try not to breathe that dark old lady scent Dad always bought her. I know she prefers Shalimar, delicate and blond in a cut glass bottle.

Funeral Home Director whispers in my ear: "We only need clothing for the part of her that visitors will see." He guides Dad and me past a parlor full of gladiola arrangements stiff in gilded Easter baskets; they look like that to me, draped with diagonal sashes – Daughter, Brother, Friends at VFW, sashes similar to the ones I had seen recently on a televised run way show of Miss Valentine's Day lingerie. There is a montage situated on an artist's easel, with black and white pictures and assorted ephemera and signatures in magic marker. I wonder how many people will come to Mom's funeral and if photo displays are a requirement.

The Funeral Parlor man leads us upstairs to a room full of half-open caskets, arranged in a semi-circle and showing off their interiors - pure white, creamy white, baby blue, one child-size with pink lining. Some are plain satin, others taffeta with tucks and pleats and various fancy gatherings each with a tiny matching pillow. They look quite comfortable. One has a crucifix stitched right into it. Rosary beads are available, on display in plastic bags in the event a family had forgotten, next to a Holy Bible on a stand. It is open to The Sermon on the Mount. Dad and I are alone now and it is very quiet. So as not to wake the dead, I smile to myself.

For some reason I think about the day when Mom and I shopped for my wedding dress and trousseau, twenty-five years earlier, choosing pale green silk for the bridesmaids and for me, antique peau de soie. Today while I examine these linings, I imagined Mom's skin against a color she herself might have chosen as Mother of the Bride. Dad studies the price tags which are tactfully displayed on the back of each coffin. He seems startled. He is looking at his watch. A needle point sign reads: Payments can be arranged to suit your Budget. Eventually he selects a mid-range oak.

Back down stairs Dad discusses the internment details. I hear the Director ask "open or closed?" as I study captured moments in a stranger's life. Mom's shoes, small, size 5 ½, are returned to me in a brown paper bag.

In our family there is no *death*. Like Inuits with one hundred ways of describing snow without actually using the word itself we say *pass on*. "You are too late. She passed on," Dad tells me at the back door.

Mom had prayed for a healing from secret blindness and in fact, some days her vision improved, creating false hope. Mom always had trouble getting the right glasses when I was a kid. Someone, probably an optometrist, brought up the subject of cataracts, although she undoubtedly denied his diagnosis. Ultimately there was no way of denying gestational diabetes caused by late-in-life first and only pregnancy at age forty-two. I was that bouncing ten-pound baby girl, producing in Mom excessive weight gain rocketing her from petite 4 to a size 16. I should have recognized this from her constant thirst and food cravings and frequent urination. And then dramatic weight loss. That was in New Jersey and I hadn't witnessed it first hand.

She finally admitted to me that her sight was gone last year when she ran over someone's puppy – that was the last day she drove. She had done a valiant job covering up the inevitable with Dad's and her sister Louisa's help. "Have the surgery, do it for me," I begged after she missed the restaurant chair and fell on the floor. I knew she would refuse insulin. "That's what Christian Scientists usually do after the cataracts are removed," the eye surgeon told us, "They don't subscribe to after-care once sight is restored." What I didn't know was that she had been in bed for two days.

"Dad, what are you saying? Why didn't you call me?" No answer. Has she gone, crossed over, no longer with us, deceased, departed, in Heaven with Jesus and singing in a choir of angels, walking in the valley of the shadow of death, but only in the shadow, anywhere but in that unspoken state of 'dead'?

* * * * *

I am standing in the kitchen of my childhood summer home, remodeled, when Dad retired, holding a carton of co-op groceries like I have done every Saturday morning for the past several months. There is sugar-free ginger ale, a pound of Vermont cheddar, bags of carefully measured rice, split peas and lentils. Every Tuesday Mom tells me what she wants. We had grown close when they moved from New Jersey but after the surgery some distance developed between us – she had her sight again but without eye drops and insulin, I reminded her, prognosis was poor. I wonder if she blamed me for unanswered prayer. I hoped that weekly contact would help us reconnect. When I deliver her order, she checks off each item on the list, and then says "Is it too early for a taste of that cheese?" I carve her a slice and she says "there's a bow tie for you and a cup of coffee waiting, I hope it hasn't gotten cold." We sit down together. I know she craves sweets and Dad still buys her chocolate ice-cream. I tell him he is killing her, but he just laughs. "That's what she wants", he said, "and that's what she gets". Today I'm in a borrowed car and too late for the Danish. The coffee's cold. I am her too late daughter.

Upstairs, the room is gray despite the sun. Aunt Louisa sits in the corner, lost in brushed velvet wallpaper, just a voice. "She knew you would come at the right time. She kept asking why you didn't come in?" her words spoken in this very room less than an hour ago brushed against my face. I sit next to her body. It's cool; her left arm is swollen and bruised; I didn't know she injured it, was it from carrying something too heavy? Auntie has no idea. Mom's much smaller than I remember and flat. There's dust on the headboard. Petals of a ghost bouquet are scattered on the nightstand around a vase with no water, and her Bible, open to the Twenty Third Psalm. It's damp where I sit. She's wet the bed, my late Mother.

"We prayed you would come at the right time."

"Did anyone actually call me?"

"Your father said he's been trying but your phone's not working."

"My phone's working just fine." I am impatient. "My car wouldn't start and I had to borrow a friend's so I could pick up Mom's order. That's why I was running late. Before that I was home and there are no messages on my answering machine."

This is not the first time I sit down next to a corpse. When I am 13, Mom and I are just leaving church and someone shouts: "Edwin's dead" - Mom's brother lives just up the street. "No, that's not true, there's no substance in matter." Mom grabs my hand and we try to outrun it. At the house, she takes me into his bedroom, we sit next to him, and she strokes his head. Every one else is crying downstairs.

"Wake up, Edwin. This is a lie, you are God's child. There is no death. Wake up."

I remember forming her words on my lips: Uncle Edwin, wake up, sit up, and do it for my Mom: but when the Coroner comes in I feel my face flush.

"I'm sorry I am late, Mom. I had car trouble." Maybe she can still hear me. I want to say, "Mom, wake up," just in case. "Sit up, let's have some of that Old Fashioned Golden Ginger Ale you love, do it for me." Her eyes stay closed. I hold her hand; kiss her ski-jump nose, smooth out her hair. I slip off her wedding band and put it on my pinky. What about those things left unsaid, secrets and pardons, the box of questions unasked? No tears. Not then.

Weeks later I'm clearing out her closet and sorting clothes into plastic bags for Goodwill. Mom's best friend Sophie Simpson gets the London Fog, and Aunt Louisa wants that turquoise robe she sent from New Orleans all those years ago, the price tags are still on it; too delicate Mom said, but I knew she wore it like that. I keep her red shoes even though they won't fit me. I sniff the salty armpit of a cotton blouse the way a cat might and the necks of shirts and jackets, a stray looking for clues to get back home. And when I inhale that old frayed scarf from Paris, Shalimar tears pour down my face.

Dirty Work

The last time I saw my half-brother Greg Jr. was the day we put our father in Epoch, the nursing home that recently opened on Cape Cod. 'Junior' as he preferred to be called would fly in from Seattle just for this purpose - he was Dad's health care proxy and his name appeared on every legal document as next of kin. This would turn out to be the second and last time I would ever have contact with him.

Junior emailed me, "You do the dirty work and I'll sign the papers."

I made two trips to Epoch while Dad was still in the local hospital just to be doubly sure it was state of the art – immaculate, spacious, no urine smell, attentive staff, food prepared by a former New York City chef. And it had a library: that would be the clincher. Dad was a passionate reader and re-reader of English spy novelist John Le Carre and I believed, and my brother agreed, that he would be content if he had a steady supply in large print and hard cover. And he could bring his favorite chair, the wicker one with a lopsided and food-stained corduroy cushion – "no I don't want any damn replacement," he bellowed- "what's wrong with that one?" Dad would have a roommate; this might be a drawback but we would face that together.

It was my dream come true, siblings planning as a team, making brother-sister decisions. I would never be an only child again or fly solo the way I had to when my mother, my (as it turned out) stepfather, and my aunt eventually needed extended care.

While I would have the job breaking the news to Dad that he could not return to his cozy studio apartment at 64 Kendall Circle in the Senior Housing complex where I brought him five years earlier, my brother would back me up. That was our plan. I wished Junior would be staying around for a few days, and I told him so, but he emailed that he would be leaving as soon as Dad was settled-in at Epoch. He didn't want anything, except maybe that brass lamp with the green glass shades, it belonged to his grandmother, he said: I could mail it when he gave me the money. I should also get rid of Dad's truck just in case he found a way to drive that old unregistered pick-up again.

Mrs. Clarke, the property manager at housing had been encouraging Dad up until now – come over to the community building for the party – and he almost went except he saw a neighbor using a walker and changed his mind. Two days ago she called me at home: "Your Dad's had a fall and he is refusing medical attention, he has a gash on his head and will need stitches. He might have a concussion. The Director has decided he's not going to be able to come back here, he needs more supervision than we can provide." When I arrived, the ambulance had already pulled up, preceded by a police cruiser. A small crowd had gathered, "Go away you damn old busybodies," Dad yelled at his neighbors, but he became more subdued, intimidated really by Officer Collins. Reassurance that I would follow him to the ER seemed to make things worse. "Call my son," he said, "he'll get me out of this mess." Dad would later accuse me of taking him out of his apartment at gunpoint.

My life had intersected with my brother for the first time four years earlier because of another emergency. Dad had been rushed to Mercy Hospital in Rutherford, New Jersey, after he collapsed on the sidewalk. Upon admittance he denied having any living relatives and it was only after he made his escape that staff discovered Junior's and my phone numbers in his wallet, forgotten in his hasty departure. He later told us didn't trust the attending Physician, describing him as a dark-skinned man wearing a turban with a monotone whisper so soft Dad couldn't hear him and then he became increasingly agitated when this cruel foreign alleged doctor threatened him by raising his voice. Also there was a crazy man in the other bed who talked gibberish. Dad then became convinced the nurses were trying to starve him to death because they only fed him clear broth and Jell-O. And as if this weren't enough, it was a Catholic Hospital. So the same day he was admitted, and when the Sisters of Mercy weren't looking, Dad got dressed, made a dash for the stairway, walked down two flights wearing hospital slippers and once out the front door, convinced a taxi driver to give him a free ride home.

Called by Mercy Hospital, my brother and I arrived at Dad's and neither of us knew the other was coming. Dad had told me a little about his son, eleven years older than I, making him about sixty: a professor of some kind or other out West, those were his words, and he wrote awful poetry and Junior should have taken his advice and stayed in airlines, he would be retired now, with a pension living on Easy Street and why he would write poems that didn't rhyme was beyond his comprehension.

My first impression of Junior was: Brooks Brothers. He wore a beige cashmere cardigan and a brown striped button-down shirt. His shoes had tassels. Except for our eyes there was nothing facial that indicated we were blood relatives. I thought to myself he must have had a strong resemblance to his mother, but I had never seen a photo of her in any of Dad's albums.

Looking for similarity, I told him I wrote poetry that didn't rhyme either. He didn't smile. As it turned out, he was a published author of distinction: two years ago he received a David T.K. Wong Fellowship and this year would be living in East Anglia on a $42,000 stipend while he completed his book on the Far East. I thought "wow."

"I hope you know what you're doing," my new brother said to me that first day we met. As well as my concerns for Dad's health, there was his recent letter: 'Christ the Redeemer, the Protestant Episcopal Church I have attended for fifty years now has an openly gay Bishop. Rutherford's gone to hell. If you come and collect me, you can have my Datsun truck, it's a stick shift. When you park on a hill; it will usually jump-start.' Later he reneged on that deal, a stroke of luck for me.

Moving Dad to the Cape would be just another daughterly task of many which I had exuberantly taken-on ever since Dad located me shortly after

Mom died. "I heard about your mother", his letter said. "She and I had a special relationship many years ago and if you want to find out more I am I your disposal" My lawyer suggested DNA, but I just knew from the crook of his nose and the line of his jaw, he was my real Dad and he came with a bonus, a brother. He was everything my other father had not been...fun, a drinker, an adventurer. He could tell stories about layovers in Cairo and Paris when he worked for TWA. He once owned an art gallery; he could give me financial advice, "I'll make you a rich woman." He suggested we move to Florida and live together; he'd buy us a big house in Sarasota. For the first two years it was almost a romance. My son hated him.

When Dad was eventually discharged from Cape Cod Hospital with 38 stitches and a slight concussion he went directly to Epoch. Junior signed the papers and headed back to his life on the West Coast, too loyal to his mother to have an on-going relationship with me, he said. Where was I when he needed me, he asked. I didn't answer, but I was thinking, probably still in High School. A pretty nurse convinced Dad to get a new cushion for that wicker chair. He refuses to speak to me, so I don't go to see him very often; he's sure I stole his Datsun and maybe he thinks I'm a spy, too. He loathes his roommate who snores at night and talks gibberish all day.

Somewhere I read this quote from John le Carre, it may have been on one of Dad's bookmarks: "The only reward for love is the experience of loving." Sometimes I picture Dad and my Mom trysting at the Biltmore Hotel in Manhattan, where I was conceived. She wore big hats with flowers, he said. I wonder if they requested the same room each time, maybe she kept the key for a few years after, wore it on a chain around her neck; it would have been brass with the number stamped into it. I wonder if they danced at the Cascades to Guy Lombardo's band. I wonder if he stood her up after she announced she was pregnant. She had her reasons for not telling me about him. I read that the Biltmore was demolished in 1981 despite protests to make way for Bank of America.

I decided not to send Junior that brass lamp with the green glass shades right away. Maybe I'll keep it, after all, it belonged to my grandmother, too, and sometimes dirty work has its unexpected rewards.

Jacqueline M. Koiner, II

The Word

I laughed the first time I heard the word because I didn't know what it meant. So when the little Australian boy with the beautiful blue eyes told me that's what I was I took it as a compliment. But as I grew up, I was unwittingly drawn to the place where I would form my most desperate friendships and it was through these alliances that I would hear the word in everyday conversation. Although I soon learned that with this word came innumerable degrading thoughts, it was still just letters; strung together by the ignorant like popcorn on a string. But then came you. You were supposed to love me as only a mother can love her drug addicted child. But instead, instead, after ten years of commitment and loyalty, love making and pain, after 10 years of caring for you as though I had only yesterday weaned you from my breast; you called me the word.

Nancy Owen Nelson

Fertility

It's January of 1980, and despite problems in my marriage, I am anxious to have a baby. I will be thirty-four this year. My biological clock is ticking. I tell my husband Warren and his response is tacit agreement. On a cold Michigan afternoon, with snow falling rapidly outside, we act on our agreement. And in the small bedroom of our rented house, enclosed against the cold of winter, I have visions of a future with my child.

By February I notice the changes in my body. It will be an early October birth, the doctor says.

During my pregnancy, Warren works long hours with the oil exploration crew. He has little interest in our home life. He refuses to change the cat boxes, despite the danger that I might catch toxoplasmosis, a parasitic disease which would be a danger to the fetus. At Lamaze classes, he falls asleep during the video of childbirth. While Warren snores, the other husbands watched intently, gently stroking their wives' bellies.

I grasp for evidence that our relationship will become more loving and cooperative; the arguments, violence, and verbal attacks continue. We are going to have a baby. What will that mean? Another life will soon join us. Things *must* change now. I hope for a new future but instead find myself pressed against the wall in our dining room, my huge belly distended even more by the arch of my back as Warren twists my arm behind me, presses his open teeth against my face, and spews foul words onto my cheek. The baby turns loops in my stomach, his feet kicking vigorously. *Can he hear my weeping?*

October 9, 1980, 12:15 a.m. I awake a few hours after an argument. I am cramping. I climb the stairs to the bathroom and find bloody spotting. The cramps are increasing. I begin to time the contractions. I call my doctor. Cramps are three minutes apart, then two minutes. I call to Warren through clenched teeth, clutching the banister at the top of the stairs. I am afraid I will fall trying to go down to wake him. It takes him a full ten minutes to wake up.

When the contractions are 1 minute, forty-five seconds apart, we leave for the hospital and drive through the chilly, early fall night to Albion Community Hospital. My rapid breathing fills the car with a white fog.

2:00 a.m. Our priest, Father Jim, arrives. I am positioned in the delivery room, a glucose IV in my arm, fetal monitor in place. Warren takes cigarette breaks from giving me ice and helping me count the breathing. Father Jim comes into the labor room, holds my hand, and we make jokes. "If I didn't know better, I'd think this was the fruit of the Garden!" I struggle to speak. "Well it is!" He says. "Bullshit!!" I gasp between birthing breaths.

6:30 a.m. Contractions are down to 1 minute, 30 seconds, but I'm not dilating. The doctor, a woman my age, monitors the contractions.

8:00 a.m. Contractions are still at one minute, 30 seconds (it's almost two hours now at this stage); my energy is waning; ice and glucose supplements do no good. Sweat rolls from my scalp and hair, my back is on fire, and my neck muscles are strained to a point of breaking, like taut ropes stretched beyond their limit. The doctor mentions a Caesarean section. Then in a moment she starts to leave the room. I clutch her arm. "Where are you going?" She replies, "To wash my hands. We're going to have a baby!"

8:11 a.m. Fast breaths, a push, a final thrust, and I hear the sounds of my son's first breaths in the outside world. He sounds like a squawking chicken. He weighs 8 pounds, 2 ounces. The nurses bath him off with warm water and lay him, warm and wet, on my breast. He struggles to find my nipple. I rest, joyful and hungry, and I ask for a cup of coffee and breakfast. It is new life, it is a miracle.

* * * * *

During the nights after his birth, I am exhausted from being wakened every hour and 45 minutes to feed Owen. All of my hopes the rebirth of this marriage are foolish. I have nowhere to go, no clear path.

On a Sunday afternoon in April, Warren watches television in his bathrobe, naked underneath. He has not showered, brushed his hair or teeth. Today Owen has an ear infection. He cries on and on, in piercing, grating screams. I ask Warren for help, to take Owen for awhile and rock him so that I can rest. I ask to change the channel to a Shakespeare play--anything might help, any kind of distraction. We argue over the program. Warren, holding a screaming Owen in his left arm, backhands me across the face with his right hand.

On that day, I admit to myself for the first time that this marriage is poisoned with violence, anger, and recrimination. Having my baby has only made the picture clearer. I must give my son a good, loving environment, where people do not raise their voices and strike out, where parents are equally and mutually respecting partners in the process of raising their child. I must do this, even if it means raising him alone.

I must leave. I apply for a teaching job in a city in my state. At the end of the summer, I receive a call for an interview.

If I get this job, I can go.

The interview proves successful. I am offered the job and I take it. In late August, I pack our clothes and divide the household items. Warren drives a truck with my part of the furniture; we move my things into a two-bedroom apartment in Westland, second floor, overlooking a lovely wooded area and a lower section of the Rouge River. This will be our home, mine and my baby's, for the next three years. As we make trips into the apartment with

boxes, clothes, and pieces of furniture, Owen stands in the playpen and
screams, sensing the tension and anxiety. That night, sleeping side by side in
the pull-out couch of a friend, Warren and I hold each another and cry.

But still, I must leave.

* * * * *

By the next summer, I am divorced from Warren. I am a teacher of
English in a community college. And most of all, I have my son. He will live
with me for twenty years.

But he will be my son for life. I will never regret my decision to have him.

* * * * *

Burr Oak Street in rural Michigan
glows with brown, gold,
yellow, orange leaves.

October 9. Pains begin at 12:15 a.m.
A cool night, bracing itself
for colder nights to come.

I know the signs, count the seconds
between each throb, electric
belly currents.

I climb steps slowly, one at a time,
brace myself, grip iron railings,
for each wave is

like a heartbeat
like an tribal drum
like an urgent call.

Outside, wet wind blows leaves
against the house. It's
almost Halloween.

At three years old I am a ghost
in white sheet, eyes peering
through ragged slits.

I moan, and my girl voice rises
through an Indiana fall night,

joins wet winds

bearing down on leaves, mostly yellow,
some orange, a damp carpet
on lawns, sidewalks.

This will be a long night of monitors
ice chips, moans, counted breaths,
dampened forehead, patted dry.

At 8:11 a.m. he will emerge,
his cries like a chicken squawking.

I will take him home. By then,
trees will stand barren of leaves.

Venetia Sjogren

My Oldest Memory

My earliest memory is of language. I have an older brother who is deaf; like other younger siblings, I mimicked everything he did, or in his case, did not do. My brother existed in a world where his nimble fingers, were his words accompanied by the expressions on his face. Being his baby sister, I too, existed in that world until I was three years old.

Brother had the most communicative fingers and animated facial expressions; we discovered the world through them. He made colors and people come alive. At the age of three, my father enrolled us in separate schools, me in a private preschool, my brother in one for the deaf. Consequently, we had to enter separate worlds. But I never forgot the first language that I was truly fluent in, wasn't the Spanish of my family, nor the English of my adopted country, but a private sign-language, between myself and my beloved brother.

Anjie Seewer Reynolds

A Story of Love and Teeth

When I'm asked what it's like to be married to a dentist, my first response is glib: I get teased for being the only parent who sends their kid to a sleepover without a toothbrush; I co-carry a school debt load as big as a house mortgage; and, I'm expected to have perfect teeth and even better breath, which, in my experience, is not always possible.

But then there's the response that's not glib, but heartfelt – as true as anything I've ever believed – and the only way I can express it is like this: I can't separate out my particular dentist *guy* from his dentist *job*. *Together*, they make him the person I'm married to.

My particular dentist guy, Mick, was once an unfulfilled twenty-eight year old manufacturing and plastics engineer who drew computerized sketches of an airplane's wing rivets for a prominent aerospace corporation. A couple years later, he designed water ski and wakeboard bindings for world class athletes. Cool enough, to be sure, but that same engineer guy would come home disappointed that he'd sat at a machine all day and had spoken to only one or two other human beings – about nothing that meant anything to him.

Then Mick got laid off, the very weekend before planes were used as bombs to take down the Twin Towers, and engineering jobs got tough to obtain. He spent six uninspired months searching for engineering work – mostly in his underwear at the computer – while I taught college courses part-time and we shared care for our infant and toddler. Desperate, Mick eventually took up work with a contractor, installing hardwoods and painting trim for another few months, work he found physically fulfilling but not ideal.

Somewhere in there, though, he observed his younger brother at work as a new dentist. Sitting in the operatory next to his brother's assistant, Mick watched carefully. He saw how the mouth was the gateway to health for the rest of the body (doctor), he watched his brother's hands move in intricate and detailed ways in a small space (engineer), and he listened to the care, banter, and concern communicated between patient and dentist (human being). In short, he immediately saw how he, too, could use his head, his hands, *and* his heart all in one fell swoop: by being a dentist. Initially, he didn't say anything about what that visit meant to him, but I'll never forget the day he pulled our old VW Vanagon off the highway and cut the engine in an IKEA parking lot. He unfastened his seatbelt and turned to me, his voice shaking, "I think I want to be a dentist."

I shivered.

Then I nodded my head like crazy. I knew he could do it, and I knew he'd be good at it. I also knew he was brave to want it, which added yet another layer of love for him in my heart. There in the van, he told me he'd considered dentistry in high school, but thought the road too long and possibly too hard. However, after watching his brother go through dental school, he reflected on how four years passed *no matter what*. Time passes whether you're doing what you want to be doing, or not. Why not take some risk and make sure time passes as you do something meaningful?

Looking at our two kids, oblivious in their car seats, Mick said, "I want to leave them a legacy they can be proud of. I want to leave a legacy of pursuing dreams – even if they seem really, really challenging."

So Mick returned to college at thirty-three, taking three full years of pre-requisite classes from the school where he'd graduated seven years earlier. For the first few months we wondered what we'd gotten ourselves into. We were on public assistance for Women Infant and Children, my part-time contract work at a college an hour and a half away was finally up, and we were out of money. I remember standing in the kitchen taking a phone interview for a bus driving job, with my toddler squeezing my knees and my baby sticking a Cheerio in her mouth she'd found on the floor. I was scared, I could barely concentrate, and I couldn't stand the thought of random hours driving an airport shuttle.

That interview, and another for a resume`-writing service, went horribly. We trusted my persistence would pay off, though, and put the word out to all our friends that we each needed work. Our friends were excited for us, even envious at times, and they looked out for us, the way people will when they want to be part of something big.

Eventually, I got a miraculous call to interview for teaching a full course-load at the university. I started a week later. Mick started a part-time job making dentures that same month.

Carefully balancing my job, Mick's job, child care shared between us, and Mick's student load, eventually we made it into the final quarter of pre-requisites. Mick scored high on the Dental Aptitude Test, filled out fifteen dental school applications, wrote a killer statement of intent (thank me very much), and earned himself a seat in the University of Pacific's three-year program, the only one of its kind in the nation.

After a mighty garage sale where we sold everything we could think to sell (mostly the quiver of free wakeboards Mick had acquired) we packed up our three and four year-old kids and moved to San Francisco for a life of school, loans, and part-time work.

Dental school was challenging and scary. We were still on public assistance and I worked part time as a pre-school teacher – so I could bring my kids – and I managed all childcare, healthcare, and household work in order for Mick to be free enough to give 100% to his studies, which sometimes felt laced with elusive requirements.

It was really hard, but it was really worth it.

Now Mick's a dentist guy, one who's just ironic enough to enjoy saying it's time to go to the dentist when it's "Tooth Hurty," and comes home from work deeply moved by the work he's done and the lives he's encountered.

Staying true to HIPAA's confidentiality code, he never tells me names or places, but his eyes often water as he tells me about hardship, victory, silliness, or gratitude he's seen or experienced in the mouths or lives of his patients. He *never* got that as an engineer. Granted, some engineers don't need it, and, admittedly, some engineers manage to get it somehow, but my guy needed something extra and dentistry is how he gets it.

So when Mick leans against the kitchen counter, a new dentist at age 41, talking to me about his work with tears in his eyes, I'm very clear about this particular *guy* who loves his particular *job,* and I hone in on that soft smile. I hold on to the memories of hardship and risk – because they make this all the sweeter – and I hone in on his lovely, if slightly imperfect teeth and his occasionally bad breath. Because, well, sometimes you just can't have it *all* -- but with a lot of determination, you can come pretty close.

Redemption

Joe Wade

Suicide and Redemption

I had been running from him since the day we met, and he finally caught me. I spent eight months hiding in the endless depths of a thousand bottles to no avail. I got on the Appalachian Trail and I ran. I ran through endless winter mountains, snow storms, ice storms, hail, and zero-degree nights. I ran through the winter into the spring, rafting rivers, surveying majestic mountain peaks, and hiding as a traveler lost in the passing millions of inhabitants in large American metropolises.

I ended up in North Carolina and made my way to the state's eastern edge. I left the mainland and disappeared seemingly unnoticed to the edge of the sand and the endless expanse of the ocean. The locals called this place the end of the world, and they were right. There was nowhere else to go. As I stood there, I witnessed a brilliant, bursting display of the sun's morning glory. It was quickly dampened and chased away by a southeast wind that brought cold sea-fresh rain and chilly gray skies. I trudged off the beach exhausted, carrying my burdensome pack, miles from the nearest campground, miles from anywhere civilized, miles from home.

It was here that I noticed him—the same greasy unkempt hair and the same cry-puffed eyes, which had turned into an angry, hellish bulge. One look into him and I knew he was clinging to the last strand-snapping thread of sanity he had left. His face was twisted by desperation, pain, and hopelessness. He was standing next to his death-black Toyota Tacoma pickup in the middle of a barren fish-cleaning station. The air around him was permeated by the odor of dead fish and ozone rain. A green portable bathroom was behind him, its door tapping a wind-driven rhythm. The sand was dirty and loose, and we were surrounded on all sides by tall green sea grass that moved and rustled with the ocean wind. A sand road cut through our patch that led to the ocean and an out-of-the-way village on the Outer Banks of North Carolina

I tried to sneak by, but he called out to me in a desperate way. The undertone was sinister. It was always sinister with him. I could not ignore him, and there was nowhere to run, so I turned to approach him. He stood on the opposite side of the truck bed. As I approached, I noticed the usual players on what, due to life experience, was becoming my unwanted field of expertise. In the truck bed was a silver .38 revolver filled with bullets that were packaged neatly into their metal jackets. Beside the gun was an inhibition-killing, half handle of tequila. The other half was undoubtedly in the man I was approaching.

"What did you say?" I politely inquired.

"Get me an armed ranger!" he replied in a rage-filled voice that was not his own. We were in a national park—asking for an armed ranger was the equivalent of asking for a police officer in the city. It was apparent to me that he wanted suicide by cop.

I knew this voice. I did not realize it then, but this was the same voice I heard not long ago. I immediately melted with compassion for the man tortured by a blinding insanity he could never understand in his current state.

"You don't want that," I replied with compassionate softness.

His eyes began to well with the tears of a man tormented by more than anyone would ever know. A flicker of hope saturated with desperation filled those dark, exhausted, and tear-flooded eyes.

I began to tell him my story and my struggle with the monster that now had him in its grip, the monster that wanted only to pull him six feet under, leaving a bloody aftermath where life once flourished.

It had been roughly a year before my encounter with this stranger on the beach when I faced the sickness that took my friend. I remember it like it like a movie. He displayed the body language that said "I am utterly defeated and cannot get up one more time." His shoulders were slumped, and his tall frame sagged against his bone structure, which looked as if it might collapse. His entire face was heavy with defeat, and his hair lay uncontrolled and greasy from the constant rubbing of his head. He moved like a ghost through the kitchen of our house, past the table where I sat, sliding by my peripheral vision. He had just come out of a rage—one of his angry protests against a world utterly cruel to him since the day he was born. He'd had enough after losing his second child. The first died from sudden infant death syndrome; the second was killed by a drunk driver. His only surviving son was scheduled to leave for Afghanistan, which, in his mind, equaled death.

I listened to his shuffled steps move farther away from me until I could no longer hear them, and I realized that this time, something was terribly out of place. Something was wrong. What was it? There was no way to place it. There was just a feeling, like the calm before a storm, as if all hell was about to break loose. I got up from my chair and headed toward the basement he had descended into, simultaneously calling out his name. I imagine the old, dirty white door must have creaked as I opened it, but I do not remember because what I saw next horrified me He was sitting there on the narrow wooden stairs. On one side of him was a stone masonry wall with sandy mortar and on the other, a dirty white wall that stopped halfway down the stairs. The shelving that ran from wall to wall left just enough headroom to walk down the stairs with a tilted head, and barely enough shoulder room to walk without brushing the walls. The floor of the basement was made of dirt, which accounted for the musty smell There were no windows; nevertheless, no amount of light could make this grave-like enclosure bright.

It all seemed much smaller with him sitting there, his back to me, one small rifle in his lap and a double-barreled shotgun pressed tightly against his forehead. His finger was squeezed against the trigger, ready to pull it all the way back.

The scene hit me so fast that it left me reeling as if I had been sucker punched by a heavyweight prize fighter. Nothing could have prepared me for this. It was the first time in my life I was absolutely speechless. I found my voice and attempted to reason with him, but his answers came calm and calculated, in a tone resigned to its fate. He knew what was to happen. This was not the man I knew but the monster that wanted his life. I will never reveal to anyone the words we exchanged; no, they will go with me to the grave. The man he was could never do what was said; it was the monster that had him in its grip that did the speaking.

Unsure of what to do, I turned to the faith I had been raised with but was always unsure of. I began to pray for him as I punched "911" into my cell phone and stood ready to push the talk button. I was not sure if it was the best idea, and before I knew what to do, I heard him whisper his name softly as if he were pleading with himself. That was the last time I ever heard his voice.

I will never forget the "pop" that echoed out of the basement. The resulting carnage that flooded my mind was the most horrific thing I have ever witnessed. The back of his head seemed to push out as if it were a ripe watermelon, and pieces of it turned and flipped into the air. It was while these pieces were airborne that I pushed the talk button on the phone, summoning 911 as I spun around and darted outside the door three feet behind me. I knew there was nothing left. He had literally blown off his head.

It was surreal to me how peaceful the outside world was. The trees were green; the air was a late-spring temperature. I had just seen death a few feet away, and here I was in small-town America, complete with white-picket fences sidewalks, and lawn mowers humming in the distance. No one was disturbed. Then the emergency operator broke the silence through the earpiece of the phone. I do not think it registered when I told him he was dead. He kept asking me to check on him, but I kept telling him there was nothing left. After a few repetitions, he seemed to understand.

There was no order after that. Police officers arrived and talked to me, fire trucks and ambulances came, and of course, the stereotypical onlookers gathered around the scene.

Soon after, I was drunk—drunk as I could be, without allowing myself to pass out, lest the monster should find me in my dreams. I began to run, run any way I could, but the monster was going to catch me. It was inevitable.

Now I was at the end of the world, facing this monster again. It was another man, but the suicidal monster was there, lurking beneath his skin—only this time, I could see him, and I knew the stakes. The story I just shared with this man softened him, and he promised that he would not shoot himself in front of me. Compassion was still there, a signature trait of humanity. The sickness was losing its grip. I noticed a Promise Keepers sticker on the back of his truck—a Christian group I was familiar with. I asked him about it, and he confirmed our common faith. I reminded him of the hope we have in God, and he seemed to crack a little more as he seesawed on the edge of utter destruction.

He waived me to the open door of his truck and showed me a picture of his kids. Tears flowed out of his eyes. Broken sobs punctured the air as he fought for breath. He rubbed his stubbly face and beat his fist against the frame of his truck as descended back into despair. The guilt of his part in the divorce seemed to be hammering his mind relentlessly. He told me all he wanted was to keep his family, but felt that would be impossible. His heart was ripping at the seams; wounds had been created that seemed to be mortal. No amount of reminding him of his children helped. The situation seemed to be one of revolving hopelessness.

I explained some research studies I had read about divorce and treatable, temporary depression that often accompanies it. Nothing I said registered, and he offered me his camper along with the keys if I would go away.

I felt I was losing again. I had no cell phone this time; all I had was prayer, so I prayed again. I decided to stay with him until he got better. I told him I was not leaving him until he was clearheaded and gave me the bullets to his gun. So we hung out and shared our pasts. He broke down several times, and I did the one thing I wish I could have done to the one I lost—I gave him a hug. This man, who was once a hostile stranger, was now a dear friend, if only for the moment.

After speaking for a while, we decided that he should go and see his psychiatrist. He got into his truck, and we drove out of there. I rode with him until he got near his psychiatrist's office.

We parted ways, closer than many people are after years of knowing each other. We had each been saved by the other. In a very serious tone, he asked, "Are you sure you're not an angel?"

"No," I replied. In fact, he never knew that he was mine, and that the monster that chased me had been put to rest as a result of meeting him. I found my peace as he drove away, and I wandered, lost in an awestruck-trance, across the sand to a nearby campground.

Madeline Davis

In the House of the Lord

"...and I shall dwell in the House of the Lord for ever and ever. Amen." These words that end the Twenty-third Psalm of David are familiar to both Christian and Jewish children. They conjure up fairy-tale visions of the marble halls, of a glorious heaven. And though Reform Judaism, in deference to egalitarianism, no longer uses the term "Lord" to describe the Almighty, Adonai, those of us who were brought up hearing these words, can still imagine a grand afterlife, overseen by a beneficent old man who would smile and welcome us to his home where we would be cared for unto eternity. It was a wonderful story for children. But we are no longer children. God is no longer "The Lord". And in many houses of worship, we gay and lesbian people have not been particularly welcome.

In early July, 1995, Wendy Smiley and I were "married"* by Rabbi Ronne Friedman, Senior Rabbi of Temple Beth Zion in Buffalo, New York. Although Beth Zion's building is relatively new, as a congregation it is very old and has included many of Buffalo's wealthiest and most influential families. I recall my great aunts talking about their Reform Temple and their religious leader, Rabbi Fink, and I shared their view of the huge old temple that stood on Delaware below North Street as a place of awe and reverence. From the time she was a child, my mother was a member of this congregation, an affiliation bestowed upon her by these same aunts who dismissed her grandfather's rantings that Reform Judaism wasn't Judaism at all, and that to be really Jewish you had to be Orthodox.

When my parents married, however, they lived on the near east side near Temple Beth David, a small Conservative synagogue with a working class congregation. This is where I went to Sunday School, won prizes for scholarship and fought with the Rabbi about the existence of God, finally stalking out of his office when he told me I was too young to understand. After that day, organized Judaism held little fascination for me. I observed holidays when friends or relatives did. I went to temple when my mother, who was especially fond of Beth Zion's Rabbi Goldberg, wanted to go. I make chicken soup and matzoh balls and tsimmis. I know a few Yiddish phrases and when I get excited I speak with a slight but discernable cadence. I have been Jewish, simply because I was born into a Jewish culture. Until the wedding.

When we finally decided to "formalize" our relationship, Wendy and I began making plans for a relatively simple Pagan ceremony in the woods, conducted by one of the elders of the women's spiritual community. We started creating the guest list and discussed at length whether family members might be uncomfortable with a Pagan ritual. During this discussion Wendy admitted that, although the idea of a ceremony in the woods sounded lovely, she had always wanted a "real wedding", meaning a traditional Jewish ceremony performed by an ordained Rabbi. The thought that we could have a ceremony with even a remote resemblance to the one that had joined our parents, and their parents before them, had never occurred to me. After all, we are lesbians. In my mind, lesbians exchange rings, pledge their love, move in together, purchase "things" together, observe anniversaries, and occasionally hold a celebration of their union in the company of friends. We do not marry each other in "The House of The Lord." This would be too much, too audacious, too presumptuous, a shondeh (shame) for the neighbors. However, it was not only my assumptions with which we were dealing. In Wendy's mind, you never know until you ask. And so we did.

Our first meeting with Rabbi Friedman went well. We knew he had conducted gay commitment ceremonies at his former rabbinate in Boston and that he might be willing to do the same for us. Ronne tried to make us comfortable in this place that represented so much to both of us. It is in places like this that gays and lesbians have felt rejected, isolated, angry and sad. The church or temple has been a place of our heritage, but not the place of our present. It is the place of our birth families, but not the place of the community in which we live our daily lives.

Knowing this, Ronne explained his position on gays and his experience with gay and lesbian congregants. And he spoke to us of Kiddushin (blessedness), the formation of that special, unique relationship we call marriage. He asked us why and how we had come to this time in our lives; what we liked and loved about each other and how we had made our decision to marry. He asked about families, friendships, our past relationships and our hopes for the future. And in the end he agreed to help with the creation of a ceremony and to perform it for us the following July.

Because my mother had been a member of the temple we were able to renew her membership and fulfill the formal requirement that would entitle us to use of the building. We both assumed that we would have a small, intimate ceremony in the Rabbi's study, away from possible criticism from the congregation. It would be quiet; it would be hidden. Wendy asked about the room. To our surprise, Ronne told us we could have the ceremony anywhere we wanted. If we wished the chapel, a lovely room that held about 150, it would be fine. But if the main sanctuary was more to our liking, that would also be available. As we entered the large, awe-inspiring sanctuary with its huge gold and glass menorah, its imposing pillars with the ten commandments inlayed in gold and mosaic, its beautiful choir loft and, of course, its exquisite Ben Shahn stained glass windows, we made our choice. Impossible as it seemed, we would be joined in this wonderful space.

The next months were filled with the requisite anxieties: how many to invite? (as the list grew in size like a snowball rushing down a mountain), had we forgotten anyone? (and of course we had), what about a caterer? (the usual pot luck was out!), what to wear? (2 tuxes? 2 gowns? 1 of each? none of the above?), a live band? a d.j.? champagne? cake? flowers? invitations? a honeymoon? Just the thought: 2 lesbians - one over 40, one over 50 - on a honeymoon. It made us laugh; it made us smile.

For the most part our families responded with joyous good will. Parents, siblings, aunts and uncles, cousins and old friends from as far back as grammar school planned to attend. It was overwhelming. Wendy's parents sent her great grandmother's Huppah (a tent covering symbolizing the couple's home) and her father gave his Kiddish cup (a ceremonial vessel used for blessings) which had been passed down from his great grandfather in Russia. My mother volunteered to read her special prayer on the Bimah (altar) and Wendy's mom read the Seven Blessings. Wendy's work friends held a pool party shower. My work friends had a luncheon. Our "Best Women" held an outdoor barbecue. More friends came to offer their services. Paul Michaels designed beautiful wedding rings, Dodie Braun arranged for magnificent flowers and with her brother and sister concocted an amazing wedding cake, Jim Strash created purple satin vests, ties and yarmulkes (skullcaps) for our outfits, and Leslie Wolff designed a very classy invitation.

The wedding was perfect; I wept from the start. The Rabbi's stories and blessings will resonate throughout our lives. Two-hundred and sixty friends and relatives witnessed the ritual and celebrated with us until midnight. We danced and sang, drank toasts, laughed and cried over and over again. And at one a.m. we drove home with a carload of beautiful gifts, tired and thrilled. Because we had not had a moment to eat any of the delicious food prepared for the reception, after getting into night clothes I prepared tuna sandwiches for us and we happily crawled into bed to relive the wedding with shared stories until we fell asleep. After an evening of strenuous revelry a traditional wedding night faded into mythology!

The next day we drove relatives to airports and trains. We kissed old friends good-bye. And, finally alone, we looked at our Ketubah, the Jewish equivalent of a combination license and written vows of commitment. Words like "my only beloved", "my lover, my teacher, my friend", "through all of our days together" glowed from the page. These were the words we had written for each other, and they were good. But there were other words. Words written for all Jewish couples for the day of their joining. "To establish a home ...where the passages of life are celebrated through the symbols of our Jewish heritage. ... A home joined ever more closely to the community of Israel."

It was done. We had been joined together in Kiddushin. For so long we had associated our sexuality with identity and pleasure, but also with disapproval and rejection. But a change had come. Although Judaism had certainly not bestowed its blanket approval, one intrepid rabbi, one brave board of directors, one forward looking congregation made space for the recognition of one lesbian couple's union. Although both of us had been in good and stable relationships, this unique experience has truly set this particular union apart. We have been accepted by the faith of our fathers and mothers into the family of those whose unions have been consecrated before the deity of our ancestors. Like theirs, this one was blessed in "The House of The Lord." And it has made all the difference.

*As of July 1995, no state in the U.S. recognized gay and lesbian unions.

Marty Kingsbury

Missing

It wasn't in the cupboard or in the sink. Not beside the tub, or under the bed. Not in the closet or under the covers or behind the toilet or in the garage. It was definitely missing.

It was a cup, a simple little coffee cup, embossed with the tall stones of Stonehenge, as graceful and brave as a cup could be. She bought it on Halloween when the stones seemed to dance in the shadows.

That summer and into the fall, when she and her love could not stop fighting, she went to England and hopped a train and rented a car. She rolled the windows with her right hand, smoked with her left, and drove through the rain and the fog on roads that wound and curled and twisted through cathedrals and fields as trees shed their leaves and the sun barely squeezed through the fog until up out of nothing, the stone towers rose like ancients beasts. She laughed and cried and gaped at eternity in that beautiful dying light.

And when she sat with her love that Thanksgiving morn, hot coffee in her Stonehenge cup, she knew that she was brave enough.

But that was then.

Now she lies on her belly, as dust bunnies dance in the morning light, hoping against the inevitable.

"Look at you, crawling around under the bed for, what is it, the fourth time? Why haven't you figured it out? You pissed me off. I broke your stupid cup. So there."

And that was how the last dream of family and future and love vanished into the smoke and shadows of what once was but had never really been.

Chantal Jules

Stilettos

Love is much like a wild rose,
beautiful and calm, but willing
to draw blood in its defense.

~ Mark Overby

I walk with a heavy heart. What an understatement. I walk with the weight of the world on my shoulders and the constant presence of guilt in my soul.

A painted lipstick smile adorns my face, deflecting any suspicion of lingering pain with a laugh and artificial happiness. The sound my stilettos make as I walk down the corridors of my empty life, tells them that yes: I'm dealing with it fabulously. A veritable pillar of strength that girl is, look how she carries herself despite her loss. Go on girl, too blessed to be stressed right?

My act is Oscar worthy, Angelina Jolie has nothing on me. My performance: flawless; the joyless depths of my eyes are my only betrayer, my personal Judas. Alas, when the audience has gone home, and the movie screen is blank, that all consuming pain comes to me again.

It never goes away, it just waits for the time when I am alone and it can again ravish me as a passionate lover devours the essence of his beloved. Yet there is nothing passionate about this lover. It engulfs my being in complete sorrow sinking its sharp talons around my heart, constricting to the point where breathing becomes unbearable. My soul has been ripped to bloody shreds of misery part of it dying when the bullet ended his life.

My hands may not have pulled the trigger but they are not without blood. I am as responsible for his death as the coward who took him from me. I failed him as his woman, as his friend as his twin flame. God gave me the gift of love and I threw it back at Him like a spoiled child throws a toy she has barely touched, wanting a better and more expensive one.

He and I were made for each other. Countless couples regale in the same sentiment of designed love, we truly fed on each other's strengths, our weaknesses, our pride and our insecurities. Ours was a dysfunctional, yet unconditional love.

As a lamed person who has lost a limb and still feels the phantom appendage, so I feel his absent presence. My heart and mind are in constant battle, my heart cannot and will not come to terms with his death. My mind is a selfish and cold thing that wants to forget. In essence that is our flaw as human beings- our hearts are hapless things that want to hold on to the past, that want to love beyond any reason. As the clichéd moth to the flame so is the heart, a glutton for pain.

As Love is our greatest attribute it is also one of our greatest downfalls. The mind on the other hand is a cold and calculating thing. It has no time for such emotions, it registers pain, tells the heart to deal with it in a timely manner and move on. The mind is the doctor, who tells you, your child has ravishing cancer and only has a few months to live at best, then goes out to play nine holes of golf with his peers. He is not content to deliver this news, but life must go on. The heart is the mother who holds on to her child's hand crying silent tears of sorrow so as not to worry him. She will never know joy again; as sure as her child will die, she too has died; killed by the words of her child's physician.

Heroin killed my Tony, and I let her. Her hold was too strong on him. Let not my words fool you, I come from the school of hard knocks. Centuries of Spanish blood flow strongly through my veins. I am not a fighter by nature; neither am I a Saint by any means. I do not enjoy indulging in violence. Yet I will beat a bitch's ass over what's mine.

That demoness named Heroin mopped the floor with me and I couldn't do a thing about it. She wanted Tony as much as he wanted her, and no matter how good the sex was, how fly my ass looked in some jeans, or how just a soft kiss from me, was enough to arouse in him the deepest lust; he always went back to her.

Not even the purest love that comes from holding your children, and hearing their innocent laughter could make him leave her. Theirs was a love/hate relationship they had going. He hated her, the way she made him feel about his self, the things she made him do to get her. But oh what a high she gave him, when she infused her sweet poison through him, he felt omnipotent, he felt as if he were God in the flesh. The ghetto Messiah and his whore Mary Magdalene. How many times did I wish him death? I cannot remember. Was I wrong to wish it? Perhaps I was, but when you work your ass off to make ends meet and you have to boil water to bathe your kids, do homework by candle light since your utilities have been shut off for non payment, you really do not feel like sugar coating things. Especially when that hard-earned green was used to snort heroin on the streets of Chicago, with other "slaves" to that poisonous bitch.

Well, after about eight years of this three-way, my mind said fuck him and the past I had with him. A thirteen-year past, a past filled with memories sweeter than honey, a past that included three beautiful children, a past of sacrifice, hardship, and the enduring true love that only a few people are blessed to have experienced.

The man who could protect me from all the fowl things in this world, just by holding me in his arms and kissing my forehead was gone. The man who thanked me with tears in his eyes for his first born son, was gone. The man who looked at me and whispered he could spend the rest of his life staring into my eyes. That man was gone. It's my turn to look into eyes. Eyes innocent from all evil and devoid of all that is tainted by this fucked up ass existence we call life. I look into the eyes of these kids he and I created in an act of pure love.

I don't want these kids to see Daddy nodding off anymore while they're playing with him. And I'm running out of excuses as to where Daddy was for the past week. So my mind tells him to get the fuck out, it's over. And this hardened west side thug cries. Cries because he knows this time I'm not playing. This time its for real, he begs saying he will get help, he will change because he needs his family like he needs air to breathe. But my mind has heard this all before and knows that if I don't do this now then I never will. Now my heart is scared, it loves him too much to be away from him, it feels it cannot go on if they are apart, so it reminds the mind of how they first met, how the attraction was so intense it was unsettling, how it felt when he did it to me for the first time, how the most simple things he did like combing the tangles out of my hair after a shower made me feel as if I were a celebrated Goddess.

The adoring look in his daughter's eyes as he spoke to her reminded me how caring he was. No magazine or TV show could ever make her feel insecure about who she was. Her Daddy always made her feel like she was the star in his world. A flawless diamond, unbreakable.

How he looked onto his son with such pride and love, knowing that the best part of him has been infused into this little version of him. That this little boy would grow up to be the man he knows has lived in him for so very long.

How he teared up as his youngest son crowned, and he held this tiny life in his massive arms, overwhelmed with how the love for this little being made him feel. Promising himself that no harm would ever come to this beautiful angel God had graced him with. And then my heart pulls a desperate move, it reminds me how I felt as I held Tony in my arms during his withdrawal, how he sobbed as the sickness over took his entire body. How I wiped his chin after the nausea would render him almost infantile. How I cried with him, telling him that together we would overcome this. How my heart ached at the sight of this mighty man, folded onto himself, willing the whole thing to just go away.

We are a game of poker, Tony and I. For the past eight yearrs he's won every round. This time around he's been dealt a bad hand. He loses in a major way. There is no breaking even its no longer just a game, the realization has set in. Now he panics. The house has come down on him hard and its time to pay up.

My mind is set, and the heart relinquishes the fight because it knows that as much as I love my man, I love my children beyond anything in the world.

Tony promises that this separation is good for him, that only the thought of never having his family can make him get help. So he goes to his mother's in Chicago. He does well for a while, but heroin can't stand the fact that there is a kindling of hope in his heart, so before that kindling grows strong enough to engulf his spirit with the fire of hope, she beckons to him and he goes to her. Except this time she will not let the situation get out of her controlling clutches, she will own him forever or she will let him go to his fate. She uses a dealer in the Ikkeys Projects, to do her bidding. Over a deal gone bad, my soul mate, my friend, a part of my essence, is shot in the head and killed. Left alone, to be found at dawn. And let me tell you, a slight bit of insanity creeps into your head when you see the lifeless stare of the father of your kids looking into your eyes as you go to identify his body.

It's been nine months since part of my life was shattered, the pain is still very real and raw. Yet I have little ones who depend on me for their survival. If Mommy doesn't get it together and go back to work, then they don't eat. So pain hides during the day, it knows if it wants to come back and feed on my soul it has to let me do the normal things that will keep us afloat.

Behind closed doors, when goodnight kisses are given and received, and the look of my babies sleeping reminds me that yes indeed there is a God, and oh what a good God he is, pain comes back. It's vicious tongue licks at my heart like a parched gazelle to the river. Guilt is pain's associate, they come hand and hand. As pain rapes my heart, guilt sodomizes my soul. A constant reminder that if I had not left him he would be at my side now, in this very bed where love was made, life created and comfort given.

The show must go on though, so in the morning after my tears have dried, I down a couple of Tylenols with my coffee to ease the pounding in my head. I shower, paint on my "happy face", with my M.A.C lipstick, put on my black 4 inch peep toe's and spray on my Escada. His favorite scent on me. My costume complete, my stilettos click their way to another performance. The tip of my Newport cigarette precariously balanced on my lips, lights the way to my eternal stage. To the theatre named My Life. Knowing that the day will be too short and that soon enough pain will be having its way with me again.

Molly Rivkin

I Care Too Much

I'm not good at arguing.

Passion overwhelms me and my argument dissolves into tears.

I can't turn this tsunami of emotion into a distilled enough, clean enough, clear enough, concise Enough, sharp enough argument to cut through the wall of misunderstanding towering between us.

I can do popular like it's my job, but I end up feeling hallow.

I'm good at things.

Cocky? Sure can be.

Everyone knows cockiness is just a lighter shade of insecurity.

I don't think it's funny when you bet your friend he can't have sex with three different girls on one Sloppy bar night.

And he does.

Using hope, desire for connection and human contact as a weapon.

Absolute acceptance: a moment when two bodies speak a language no tongue ever could.

An instant of body and heart connecting in a way brain could never understand.

Making sex filthy.

I'm too sensitive to be around your friends.

I wouldn't like their jokes about women.

Why do you?

Misogyny is old, but not weak,

Seasoned, but not wise.

Passed down from one generation to the next like a disease.

Infection spreading from locker room to bar room;

From history book to employee handbook;

From cheer squad to police squad.

TV so infected, it writhes on its deathbed.

Symptoms range from thong underwear for little girls, to the 1 in 6 women who are raped in their Lifetime.

My love, my ideas bubble and spill from me uncontrollably.

I'm fragile with hope, often crumble completely, but always rise from the dust.

Stronger this time.

Not scared anymore.

Not afraid to rush at your wall of logic with my tsunami of emotion.

When I am knocked back again, I can feel my heart beat and I know who I am.

I care too much.

Helen Peppe

Predators

The summer I was twelve I made phone calls in secret after the *Lewiston Daily Sun* arrived each afternoon. I waited until my mother was up in the garden and two of my five sisters were sneaking around the neighborhood. I scanned the classifieds quickly: Dialing a number and racing down the hallway, my heart beating scared beneath my ribs. I stretched the cord long so that none of its loops remained, risking a static-filled connection over being caught by my mother.

I tried to sound older, attempting confidence I didn't own. "I'm calling about the horse you have for sale," I said. I rarely knew the breed. The classifieds cost by the word, and the backyard horse owners of Maine, if the trash in the woods was any indication, reserved their pennies for beer, cigarettes, tires, and ammunition.

The response was usually nothing more than a grunt, forcing me to talk on center stage, trembling in both muscle and voice. I chose the least expensive horses and didn't ask why they were for sale or what kind of rider was required—beginner, intermediate, advanced, English or western—or even if the horses were healthy or above kicking and biting. I didn't know enough to care. My second question was always the same: "Would you be willing to take payments?" I paid my mother each week for grain to feed my four rabbits, which meant I hadn't seen my fifty-cent allowance in months, but I had a babysitting plan that would bring in extra money for a horse. "10 yo gelding $350 or BO" would send my heart pumping blood wildly to my ears.

"What kind of payments?" I would be asked, suspicion wrapped around each syllable.

Then I'd take a big breath to steady my voice and list my future assets quickly before being dismissed.

"I could give you seven dollars a month and a down payment of ten dollars, maybe a little more," I answered, although I didn't have the ten.

"What money are you going to have left to feed my horse?" one man asked.

"I have grass and water," I said, my voice wobbling. "I'll have hay."

"My horse is fond of his oats, honey. Give me a call when you're earning more." Then the sound of the dial tone, flat and dull as if life had been sucked from the line.

After the fourth week of sneaking phone calls, a woman said, "Do you have a pasture?"

"Yes." I held my breath, waiting.

"I don't want to sell my mare. I'm just looking for a winter home," she said. "I'm going through a divorce, but I don't want to give up everything. Where do you live?"

My directions included the breeds of tied dogs in front of houses she'd pass, and the size of the hills. "It's the dead end side of the old through road to New Gloucester," I finished.

Silence, then, "I'll bring her over tomorrow morning."

I pressed the receiver tight against my ear thinking I'd heard wrong. Nothing ever happened that quickly in my life except loss of patience. Sweat settled in the crook of my elbow and spewed from my palms. I could feel my scalp tingle beneath my long hair. All my air was gone and my knees quivered. My brain wasn't sure it understood.

"Is that an okay time?" she asked. "Will you be there?"

"Yes," I managed to say, my voice higher and smaller than usual.

She said "Bye" and I gripped the receiver in both hands. The mirror that I liked to watch myself in as I talked still hung at the bottom of the stairs, the pile of magazines and ripped picture books still sat in the basket beside the stand beneath the mirror, and the large potted cactus on the stand itself was there as always, but I saw nothing, and nothing seemed real. Was it possible that tomorrow I would have a horse to ride, a horse all for me? Then panic flipped through my center. The horse would arrive in the morning, and I hadn't yet asked either parent if I could have one.

First I pursued my father who could be pushed to say, "yes" because he barely listened to questions before answering them, but today, not looking up from the jumble of rotor tiller parts on the ground at his knees, he said, "Go ask Mamma."

Plea upon plea tumbled out in my desperation to convince my mother that a horse would benefit her, too. I forgot how the barn scared me at night. I forgot about the howling coyotes and the death screams of small prey. I stood there that August afternoon and promised without considering the below-zero dark mornings and evenings by myself in the barn before and after school. I didn't see myself pushing a wheelbarrow full of manure, hay, and shavings through the deep snow, wind blowing against me, and I didn't see myself outside, wild animals loose and noisy in the heavy black that was night. All I saw was a slide show of feeding, grooming, leading, and riding events.

"Don't think I have time to go out and clean stalls," my mother's voice rose as she slapped dirt off her gloves over the flowers. "You don't do what you're supposed to and that horse will go right back where it came from." And even though she pointed her gloved finger at me in warning and pressed her lips into a tight line, anticipating my failure, I realized with a rush of happiness that impacted my chest with a foreign wallop, that tomorrow, a horse would be mine.

A woman in her latish twenties, hair un-brushed, lank with oil, eyes darting a little crazily, rode a chestnut Standardbred mare into the yard, trailed by a red Doberman. I was raking up messes around the doghouse.

The woman jumped down off the horse's back and handed me the reins. Her dirty jeans wrestled with her rolls and struggled to contain her wide hips.

"Are you the girl who called me about Duchess?" she said, looking around as if it couldn't possibly be me. "Heidi?"

Standing barefoot in the short grass, my dirty toes digging into the earth, the fact she can't remember my name makes me feel insignificant, "Yes, but my name's Helen." I reached out toward her horse.

"Sorry, you look like a Heidi. I'm Paula."

What does a Heidi look like I think? What does a Helen?

"You babysit my son once or twice a week and you can keep Duchess through the fall and winter," she explained, her hands resting on the handles of flesh that were her sides. "I may come by and ride here and there." Her dog raised its leg and peed on the lowest rung of my orange play gym before heading toward my dog Daisy, who was barking at the end of her run.

"My little boy's two," the woman spoke loudly above the noise. "His dad and me don't get along, but he's a good kid and shouldn't give you any trouble."

I questioned silently why she gave me information about her son when I wanted information about her horse.

"I live three miles through the woods that way," she said, turning to point to the old tote road that paralleled our garden near the woodlot.

I nodded, unable to find words, even those as primitive as "uh huh." I couldn't stop looking at Duchess's gentle brown eyes, the blaze beneath her forelock. I couldn't stop my hands from caressing her neck.

"Grain her if it gets too cold. Fifty pounds of sweet feed should last you a while. Get in at least 125 bales."

I agreed, not knowing what too cold was, having no idea where I'd get he hay.

"Duchess moves pretty fast. Be ready," she turned and walked away. Halfway down the driveway, she bellowed words I couldn't understand.

I started, my heart picking up speed. What had I done wrong? The dog ran by me in a blur of red muscle, and I exhaled in a whoosh of relief. Then they were gone.

From the house I could hear the whine of the Eagles singing "Hotel California," indicating my parents were anywhere but inside with my sisters. I took off the western saddle that was too big for me and dropped it with a thump onto the ground before using the play gym as a mounting block and slipping onto Duchess's sweaty back. I relished the warmth of her fur, the reality of it against my naked legs. I lay across her neck and hugged her. Coarse strands of reddish mane rubbed my cheek and chin. In seconds, I loved her with all the power I had to love.

Thin and bony, her spine pressed the seam of my shorts uncomfortably against my crotch. She tore at the grass as if she were angry at it. I pulled on the reins to raise her head, and she trotted a few steps forward. I directed her across the yard to the city-terminated road that continued beyond my house, past the cemetery, my father and sister said was haunted, past all of that which usually terrified me.

I rode the three miles, thick woods on each side of me, onto Meadow Lane in New Gloucester, rocking gently side to side, lost in Duchess's rhythm. I let the reins hang loose, and she grabbed at the leaves of bushes with her teeth as we passed. Newly alive, as if I heard the sounds of the birds, the tree groans, and the breeze in the trees for the first time, I especially loved the sound of hoofs on the gravel and Duchess's air blowing through her nose. I felt like an Indian, a girl and her horse alone in the woods, but not really alone. There were predators: coyotes, coy dogs, bobcats, deer, moose, and smaller animals were all around me, unseen. There were rumors of bears.

With each hoof step deeper into the woods thick with low-lying junipers, choke cherry bushes, young maples and pines that encroached on the narrow gravel road, I imagined the animals that might get me if I didn't have Duchess to keep me safe. I felt the tight grip of my parents loosen and something I can describe only as possibility and happiness, a release in my chest that made me breathe fuller, easier.

That Saturday, after a few hours of traveling the farthest I'd ever been away from home without my family, I returned to the tantrums that included long rants at my sisters, verbal and sometimes physical. Their conversations beat time with the seconds of the day, always ending where they began, nothing resolved or forgotten. I thought I would know what insanity truly was if I spent one more minute listening to my mother complain about a daughter who had married a dumb Frenchman, or another who was a whore, or a about son who threw threats of God's anger into all of his sentences because he thought he was better than everyone else, or how a black woman at Sears and Roebuck had snubbed her.

* * * * *

Terror preys on my mind each night I feed and groom Duchess in the barn alone. I can hear the coyotes yip, howl, growl and fight with one another almost as if they are outside the barn door. I tell my mother that I'm scared, and she says I knew what I was getting myself into when I asked for a horse. She's stressed herself, has her own worries and I am sorry for her even as I am sorry for myself. One sister, the pretty one, is fourteen, skipping school, smoking pot, and sneaking around with boys. The next sister up from her, the sad one, is sixteen and her baby is due in a few weeks, an even older sister, deserted by her husband, is pregnant and a single parent with her toddler daughter. My psycho brother-in-law keeps running off and their two children live with us on and off. Rightfully explosive, correct when she screams, "None of you can be trusted. All tramps running around with hooligans and riff-raff. I raised you better than this."

My mother is worn and tired.

She is deep in the midst of menopause, in the midst of internal and external life changes that overwhelm her, that would overwhelm anyone. That she has allowed me to keep Duchess another year during the chaos of raising the last three of her daughters is miraculous.

I am still the good daughter, the one she can set before my sisters as an example. I earn money to pay for Duchess by babysitting just as I'd promised.

* * * * *

Cold crept into the days, stealthily, beginning small, just as hunting season started with birds and rabbits in October and ended with bucks November: first a frost then ice in Duchess's water bucket each morning. I needed to buy grain, more bales of hay. I was always on the lookout for small jobs that paid. I would do anything except help cut up deer.

Ron, my brother's hunting buddy and a friend of my parents, asked if I would like to earn some money babysitting his son. I agreed enthusiastically, hoping since he was rumored to be wealthy that he'd pay better than my adult siblings.

I rode in Ron's truck the thirty minutes from the outskirts of Auburn to his on the outskirts of Lewiston. He talked to me as he would to an adult about himself and his overweight moody wife. Having grown up with five sisters, three brothers and an overly burdened mother in my home, I assumed ill-temper was an innate female characteristic and wasn't sympathetic as much as surprised that Ron didn't know this himself, being twenty six years old. We arrived to his house and went into the living room to wait for his wife and son to return from errands.

"To be honest," he said, "I only stay here because of my son. I'm miserable."

I looked around the dark apartment cluttered with candles and hanging crucifixes. I wouldn't want to live there either and was certain a toddler wouldn't change my mind. When I heard my brother talking to my parents about Ron's inheritable riches, I pictured him atop mountains of gold coins like Scrooge McDuck in the Warner Brothers activity book I colored with my niece. I did not picture him here.

"I don't love my wife," he said lowering his voice as if it were a secret although where I came from, if you didn't like someone, you told him or her frequently.

"I'm happier now, though," he said, his bulging eyes sad. "Do you know why?"

His breath, thick with a hot smell, closed in on my face, so that I could see the roots of his beard. My nose struggled to find an opening of clean air just as my brain struggled to understand what he was saying, what he was doing. I edged away to breathe.

"I know you're young, but you seem so grownup." He squeezed my shoulders with his fat arm. "I'd like to be your secret boyfriend."

He likes *me?* I thought. *Me?* I didn't want to look at him. His beard and stink were too close. The room was too small, too Jesusy.

"I want you to keep what I say just between us until you're older, and I can talk to your parents." He pressed his thigh against mine. Surely I would suffocate with all of him so close. He hugged me.

I wasn't used to all this touching and my body fought it.

What do you want me to do?" A strong New England work ethic flowed in the blood that pumped through my veins.

He whispered into my right ear: "I'd like you to stroke me."

Partially deaf from repeated ear infections, I wasn't sure I heard correctly and didn't know if I should say: "what?" or "pardon?"

Ron stood and unzipped his pants. My mind couldn't believe what my eyes saw. Ick took root in my stomach.

He held his penis out to me as if it were a gift or a treat, and fear at breaking my mother's rules settled into my brain beside niggling curiosity.

"Touch it," and he took my fingers and placed them around his growing erection, moving beneath me like Daisy did, if my hand was near but not patting her.

The skin of his penis was surprisingly soft, almost like Duchess' nose. In seconds, it proved as unpredictable as my mother's mood, and the tiny mole near the top expanded like a spreading stain.

"Squeeze just a little and move up and down," Ron whispered. "You're doing it exactly right. You're doing great."

I wished he wouldn't whisper. I needed to hear the instructions clearly, but I caught the tone of praise and felt a glimmer of pride.

He began to groan softly, and his eyes closed, just as his penis and face changed color. "Keep going. Don't stop. Don't stop."

Now this was the type of work I understood: made to do it after I tired. Without any warning I could detect, his penis squirted into his underpants, stopped, and squirted again as if it couldn't make up its mind. Surprised and slightly distressed because I had no idea from my time spent staring at half-naked men in Sears and Roebuck catalogues that penises did this sort of thing, I jumped back to disassociate myself from the mess.

There was the sound of car doors slamming and Ron hobbled away, a white drip hanging from his thigh.

"Say nothing," he said over his shoulder on his way to the bathroom, jeans around his knees. My mind was too busy pondering penises to say anything.

Plump with tired brown hair, Ron's wife entered. A blond two-foot-tall kid hung from her hand. She eyed me to how my mother looked when she suspected I was the reason there were no chocolate chips left.

"You're the youngest sister? The one with the horse?" she asked abruptly, rather rude, I thought, for never having met me before.

"I guess."

"What do you do with Ron when he visits?"

"Nothing." My practiced answer to all questions asked in this tone.

"Does he visit with just you or with your parents?"

"I don't know, both, I guess," Then I pretended an interest in her son to distract her, squatting down to his eye level, "What do you want to do tonight?" I asked enthusiastically, all the while feeling like I'd done enough.

Ron poked his head in the room, avoiding my eyes, "You ready?" he asked his wife, and then retreated before he found out.

I didn't see Ron again until he drove me home two hours later. "Are you hungry? We could stop for a pizza."

Was he actually offering me *real* pizza? He drove into a nearly empty parking lot. The clock on his console glowed 10:30.

"What do you want on it?" he asked me after we'd found a booth in the near empty Pizza Hut.

"Just cheese," I answered, smiling big because I was ecstatic over the Pepsi the waitress had just given me.

"I've been thinking a lot about you," he said. "I'll be up tomorrow after work. I'll tell your mother I need you again for babysitting."

My mind hadn't gotten past the Pepsi and pizza. I looked around to see where the waitress might be.

I gorged myself sick with cheese and carbonation.

Back in the truck I wanted to lie down and hug a stomach that felt like it would burst from the pressure of grease and gas much like the wolf's stomach must have felt after the mother goat filled his stomach with seven stones.

Ron reached over and placed a ten-dollar bill in my lap, squeezing my thigh gently, before returning his hand to the steering wheel.

"The ten's for babysitting."

Ten dollars? Pizza? Pepsi? Penises? My mind couldn't take it all in. My allowance was a dollar and that was a recent increase from fifty-cents, and I hadn't seen it since I began to lease Duchess.

We reached the four corners before the last half-mile up the hill to my house. Ron didn't turn onto my road, but parked off to the side, so that branches reached out to touch his truck, scraping and squealing in the black that surrounded us. He pulled me over beside him.

"I loved what you did earlier. Want to try it more?"

There was more?

He unzipped his jeans, and I understood it had been a hypothetical question similar to when my mother asked if I wanted to sweep the floor. He pushed my head down and told me to open my mouth.

"I think I love you," he said, caressing my head. "Someday I'll marry you."

I tried not to think of the steering wheel pressed into my shoulder, the strain of my bloated stomach, the odd brown mole I'd seen earlier, or the last time he'd peed. If I allowed myself to picture these things, think them through, I would throw up. I had no choice but to disappear inside my head to the place I reserved for when I got in trouble and dentist visits, a place of existing without thinking, a place safe from reality. Not once did the word "no" seem a possibility.

* * * * *

I'd overheard many fights about inappropriate behavior. I knew necking was trampy and good girls always kept their clothes on. Letting a guy see or touch your breasts meant you were a whore and got you smacked with a broom. Although by twelve, I'd heard the words "penis" and "vagina" in school health class, the words and the parts were as foreign to me as they were taboo. When Mrs. Thurlow pointed to a medical illustration of a vagina, I didn't believe that all girls had them and was surprised and frightened when that night I sat in the tub and discovered I did. It was like having a hole in my stomach. My body flushing with heat in the three inches of tepid water where I bathed and washed my hair, I worried that something would get inside if I wasn't vigilant.

I'd spent the first twelve years of my life trying to be good. I barely had any breasts, and I hadn't yet disappointed my mother too badly, so I decided to tell her about Ron the next day even though I worried I'd be punished. In the wicker rocking chair, my lookout spot, I waited for her to come into the kitchen, which she soon did, my father behind her.

"I need to tell you something," I rushed before anyone could leave. My stomach trembled in panic, the secret at the back of my throat. They paused, my father in transit between the kitchen and the cellar, my mother collecting mugs for tea. My plan was to introduce the topic and add the penis component only after I saw how they reacted to Ron confessing his love for me.

"Well, tell me," my mother said. "I've only got a minute."

"It's Ron," I blurted, voice shaking. "He says he loves me, wants to marry me when I'm eighteen. He's going to get a divorce."

"Poppycock," my father said, which sounded like puppycock. At the same time my mother said, "Oh piffle wiffle."

"He does not love you. I don't have time for this nonsense," my father muttered and went down to the cellar. "Tell me when tea's ready," he yelled up.

"Daddy's right," my mother said. "Just behave yourself and stop being so ridiculous." She turned away to fill the mugs with water.

My face flushed warm with embarrassment, and the shame that had sat in a corner of my brain all day grew in size like the Grinch's heart when he heard the Who's of Whoville sing. Why, I wondered, did they think it so ludicrous that a man could love me?

Ron increased his visits to almost daily. He would arrive at 4:30 in the afternoon and go out to the barn with me to help clean my horse's stall. He plowed a path to the manure pile because he saw how difficult it was for me to push a full wheelbarrow through the snow that fell heavy the December and January. He carried buckets of water, hay bales and offered his company and attention. I did whatever he asked because I didn't want him to stop being with me in a barn where I was certain predators, having nothing to do but prey, waited patiently to catch me alone.

With Ron standing at the stall gate watching, I chucked manure into the wheelbarrow without feeling the need to turn and see what was behind me, the thing I imagined waited until I stopped paying attention before it attacked. As I shoveled, Duchess munched hay, and Ron listened to me talk.

"People don't need meat," I said. "They really don't. There's no need to kill and slaughter so many animals."

Ron's eyes intent on my face, he said, "I never really thought about it."

"What do you think it'd be like to be a deer grazing in the field, look up for a second at a strange noise or smell, and then boom? Deer don't die instantly, you know. My brothers follow the blood trail and sometimes they never find them."

"I don't much like hunting either," he said.

When Ron wasn't there, I sprinted to the barn in over large boots, spilling well water. I slammed the planked door against the endless black that reverberated with the howls and yips of coyotes, and my body felt wound, ready. Any strange sound sent pounding blood hard though my body and my feet racing to the door.

Only two of my eight sisters and brothers lived at home, and gone were the years when we had sheep, cows, pigs, and chickens. With dark arriving in the late afternoon, Ron excused himself from conversation with my mother and followed me out the door.

I thought if I treated what he asked me to do like just another chore it would relieve the darkness that lived inside me since that first night. When he touched me, I stood or lay unresisting, confused by the pleasure when I was angry and uncertain. If I was detached, hidden within myself, I could protect the real me by shutting myself tight inside my head.

When divorce proceedings began, Ron didn't need me for babysitting, but told my mother he did. Moving into a motel room about ten minutes from my house, he waited outside my school, at the bus stop and drove to my siblings' homes if I took care of their children at night.

My mother wouldn't let me stay home alone or spend the night at Mindy Parker's, my best friend from school, but she allowed me to go with Ron.

Anger against her grew. I wondered over and over again how my mother couldn't know. "Oh, piffle wiffle," repeated itself in my brain when Ron asked me to touch him. "Poppycock," my father's voice thrummed in my thoughts when Ron promised that, as soon as I turned eighteen, he would marry me.

* * * * *

Ron knocks on the door of my sister's in-town apartment. I am babysitting; my niece is asleep.

"Happy birthday," he says, entering the tiny living room, hugging me. I am used to the touching, no longer flinch. He holds a wrapped box. Surprised and nervous, I worry we'll get caught.

"Now that you're thirteen, I can tell my friends I'm dating a teenager," he says. "This birthday makes all the difference."

Yesterday I'd been twelve; today I am a teenager. Ron had given me a chamois shirt for Christmas and this day the box holds a silky maroon sweater. I wonder how I'm going to get it home without my mother asking where it came from.

"Try it on," Ron says. "I want to see you in just the sweater." I undress, and before I put the soft fabric over my head, Ron pulls me to the couch. "You're getting a little chubby," he says. "You should watch that."

Suddenly I don't like him, forget I need him for the barn. He's now like everyone else, mean and unfair. Besides he is the one who bought me all the pizza, the candy, the soda, and he is the one who is actually fat, his large stomach casting a shadow on his feet. Like any thirteen year old, I sulk.

"Let's just see if we can do it," he says.

"Do what?" I say flippantly, but really don't know.

He takes his pants off and presses me to the couch. I feel his penis, already hard bumping between my legs. I'm surprised by the heat, by how heavy he is. Maybe he is the devil.

"Just hold still," he says and pushes. I tense and wiggle away. Suddenly he's abrupt and announces, "It's not going to work," as if I've failed. In seconds he is dressed and gone. If this is sex, it isn't at all worth the amount of yelling that has gone on in my house for the last thirteen years.

Two days later my mother found the sweater.

"Where'd you get this?' she said holding it up in front of her where it shimmered in the light coming from the sewing room window.

"Ron gave it to me for my birthday."

"When? I didn't see him."

I was the youngest in a family of proven thieves and liars.

"Just before he left last week."

Lips pressed into a line, she folded the sweater and placed it on the table where she was folding laundry. I never saw it again.

That winter Ron met me whenever and wherever he could. Often he took me to his motel room, talked about wanting to eat my cherry. Thirteen years of craving hot fudge sundaes, eating cherries meant only one thing.

He wanted to show me off to his friends, took me to their apartment late at night, leaned against the wall, while talking to the man who sat in an armchair, a woman on his lap. Beer bottles cluttered the end table near them, and I wondered how someone could drink so much and not have to pee. I stared in confusion as the woman placed her hand on the man's penis through his jeans, rubbing him. They were breaking all my mother's rules. He pressed upward into her, and Ron smiled as he conversed with them as if a woman caressing a man's erection through his jeans in the company of friends is normal. Even my sisters knew you hid to do these things. He pulled me to stand in front him and grabbed my hips, and pressing his pelvis into my bottom. I could feel his hardness against me. In the truck a few hours later he would pull over onto a dirt road and ask me to stroke and lick him, tell me that he had been so aroused pressing himself into me in front of his friends that he'd almost come. Suddenly I felt powerful.

I had two lives, and fatigue wrapped itself around both of them. I went to school each day and pretended I was good, morally irreprehensible. Fear of being found out pushed me to work harder at schoolwork, pushed me to be friendlier. If I got A's and had a lot of friends, then no one would ever know my secret.

My English teacher said, "You're nothing at all like your sisters," and shame waved through my center because I was exactly like my sisters.

Voted the most popular, the most likely to succeed, the best artist, awarded a certificate for outstanding achievement in English, nothing could ease the mountain of lies I teetered on.

One Sunday in March, Ron's sister visited my brother. She sat beside me on the couch where I was memorizing Greek Gods and Goddesses and there Roman equivalents for school. Sitting there, reading about Hera being cheated on, the unfairness of it all, caused fresh anger to writhe up from my gut into my brain, making me think my head would split open only instead of Athena, all my secrets would escape and smother me.

"How are you doing?" Ron's sister asked.

Possibly she was simply being polite, thought I'd say "fine" on automatic as so many people do and continue to read mythology. Instead before she could lose interest and leave, I blurted. "Ron makes me do things."

"What's he done? Tell me," she said instantly fierce, serious, genuinely concerned and grabbed my hands in hers. Her body was tense, her blue eyes focused tight on my brown ones. I collapsed into sobs thinking I wouldn't survive the tumult of distress.

Barely able to talk through the tears, I told her everything about her brother.

"I'm so sorry," she said.

Someone was sorry. I cried harder.

"This isn't the first time," she said. "He can't seem to control himself around young girls."

Through my agony, I didn't know whether to feel relief or hurt that I wasn't special. Ron had told me that he loved me that I was the only girl he'd ever really loved.

I heard my mother's footsteps then there she was in the living room doorway, arms akimbo, glaring, "What's going on?"

Ron's sister stood up, "Nothing," then back at me. "I'll take care of it," she said and walked around my mother who continued to stare, lips clamped, eyes narrowed.

The next day Ron was parked outside my school. My brain couldn't take in the fact that he was there. I'd been so sure it was over.

"Let me drive you home, and then we'll sit for a bit," he said, his forearm resting on the rolled down window of his truck. I knew what "sit" meant.

Neither of us spoke. I was sullen, my schoolbooks lined square on my lap, thinking of what his sister had told me about the others. Ron joked and squeezed my thigh in an attempt to get me to talk. He was dealing with a young teenager however, and I sat rebelliously in silence, rolling my eyes each time he looked at me. Up the last hill, down on the other side to the four corners where Ron always turned off, but this afternoon my parents' blue station wagon sat there. First, relief hovered in my consciousness. They were here to save me, but then I saw their expressions behind the windshield: their expressions of rage, aimed at me. Slamming the car door, my father walked to the passenger side of Ron's truck.

"Get into the car!" he ordered. I did, trembling, wondering what he would say to Ron, what Ron would say to him, but my father only waved across the hood, and Ron maneuvered the truck in a tight u-turn and drove away. My parents didn't speak to me the half-mile home. In the house my father threw his cap on the fridge with a violence that sent it skidding over the other side to the floor.

"You god-damned slut, what were you thinking?" he shouted just as he picked up my mother's Danielle Steel paperback from the kitchen table and threw it at my face. When it missed, he stomped his foot in fury and flung *Better Homes and Gardens* magazines off the kitchen table onto the floor, stomping through the kitchen in his fury.

"I tried to tell you!" I shouted. "You didn't believe me!"

"You didn't tell us," my mother said. "We found out through his parents. Ron has enough problems with his divorce. He doesn't need you making things worse," she sobbed. "How could you do to this me? Now how are we going to face Ron?"

Watching her face contort with emotion I understood that much of her grief was caused by the discovery that her last child was not the good one or the smart one she had imagined, and, in that, our loss was the same.

*****

The next spring, at the end of eighth grade, I went to my brother's and Ron's sister's wedding reception. I brought a boy from school as my guest. Ron brought a girlfriend. I felt sick at the sight of him, another woman on his arm, pictures of what we did flashing in my mind. I wondered if his girlfriend knew, if they did all the same stuff. Walking up to me as the band played, he took my hand, and pulled me aside, and I thought George looked like a little boy beside Ron and, then realized, he was.

"I've missed you," he said. "How have you been doing?"

"Fine." I didn't know what to say or where to look. I was afraid my mother would see us and yell, call me a tramp in front of everyone.

"Dance with me."

Just like the year before, I did as I was told and he hugged me to him in a waltz. I could feel the shape of him through his thin slacks. When the song ended, George was gone. I found him in the parking lot.

"Why'd you ask me to come with you if you like that old guy so much?" His voice choked in his throat with accusation. New guilt layered onto old guilt, layers and layers of guilt that would remain with me, in the part of my brain where these things like to live as if a host to images of shame, embarrassment, humiliation, despair and mortification.

I wonder now if the reason I cringe when I remove my clothes in front of my husband is based on that long ago day when Ron called me chubby. If the reasons I avoid dirt roads and think cheese pizza and Pepsi are nauseating result from those late fall and winter nights with Ron. I wonder, too, if the reason I avoid friendships, am introverted and place my trust and love in few humans, but many dogs can be traced back to Ron.

What I don't have to wonder, what I know, is why I feel heaviness settle into my legs and arms when I hear a man speak with a Franco-American accent, and why I suspect men of mistreating young girls. I know the source just as I know why when I see any young girl, I assume no one is protecting her, listening to her.

*****

Eighth grade ended and summer arrived. I met a teenage boy while riding Duchess. He walked alone on Meadow Lane in New Gloucester.

"Want to ride with me?" he asked, blocking the sun with his hand as he looked at my face. His brownish blond hair sparkled in the sunlight. "It'll only take a second for me to saddle my horse. I live over there," he pointed to a crumbling house and barn.

"Sure," I said, although I'd never ridden with anyone. I followed him down the road and across the field and waited while he went in to tell his mother. In a few minutes, he came out followed by a heavy older woman in a housedress and stretched moccasins that gaped at each side of her pale feet. I recognized her meanness, the clenched teeth behind the pinched lips, the jerky motions that spoke of barely held rage. The boy—he might have been fourteen— shrank to thinness beside his mother's aggressive bulk. Staring up, where I sat on Duchess' back, he avoided my eyes.

"Ma says she has to saddle Betsy herself. Can you wait?"

The woman looked over at me, her short hair tight to her head, her doubting eyes assessing my shorts and tee shirt, my bare feet. What could she tell by looking, I thought? Could she see that there had been a man in my life who asked me to do things that I knew were wrong, but did anyway? Did I look like a bad influence? I felt myself cave inward. I wanted to hide from her searching eyes.

"I don't have time for this," she said to her son, her mouth biting each word, separating them as if she were speaking to an intellectually challenged child. "Always, you slow me down with your wants. I have things to do, too, you know. Why do you need to ride with this, this"—she looked around as if seeking the correct descriptive from the air—"this girl, anyway?"

Quick steps to the unpainted grayed out barn, slamming doors, tossing the saddle to the wooden bleached planks. Was there color that day? I remember the sun on the boy's hair, the catch light in his brown eyes, but after that everything is a dull gray except for Duchess' chestnut coat, and the green grass. In this memory, I see myself slide off my mare's safe back and lead her away from the open barn doors to let her graze, wishing I hadn't followed this boy whose name I would never remember.

"Don't just stand there," his mother shouted. "Get the curry comb. Can't you do anything right?"

I moved farther away to where I could hear only the rise and fall of the voice, but no words. Why had I agreed to ride with him? What was I doing here in a yard with strangers? I rode to enjoy Duchess' company away from bad tempers and judgment. Why had I felt a pull toward this boy? Had I been seeking companionship?

At my side, Duchess ripped big chunks of grass from the earth, snorting in loud staccato bursts as she moved her nose over the square of lawn we stood on.

Finally the boy appeared on his horse. I noticed that his bare legs, although dirty, were covered in thin short hairs as if he were sprouting. His mother led him like a baby. Humiliation has no cap, I thought as I maneuvered Duchess away to a bowed weatherworn picnic table, stood on the bench, and slipped my bare leg over her back. Smiling in my direction, the boy rolled his eyes, seeking a shared connection with me to dispel the tension.

"What did you just do?" his mother's voice sudden and sharp, rose acid and dangerous up the octaves. How many times had I heard those very words spoken in my house? Reliving this scene, I ask myself uneasily, how many times I have said the words myself to my own children. Back then, my insides tightened as if readying for assault. I could see the mother's spit spray out toward her son, hear the rasp left by cigarettes. Like poison, I thought.

"Do you dare mock me in front of this tramp of a girl you found?"

I had known the label was there between us, waiting to exit the woman's mouth and find its home on me. Before I could prepare my seat, my handmade reins, Duchess spun on her hind legs and took off at a gallop across the field, back toward the old gravel road. Her legs pumped and her hoofs pounded. She ran away with me hanging onto her neck. I'd always ridden her bareback with only a halter, through the fields, the woods, on the roads. Never had I lost control of her. The boy would think I, too, was against him.

My heart thumped in rhythm with Duchess's legs. She didn't break to a trot until we reached the woods which no longer made me think of predators but safety. Sweaty, breathing hard, Duchess blew out dust into the air through dilated nostrils, and I wished that I, too, could rid myself of all the irritants in one great release of breath.

I unhooked my arms from her neck and sat up. I hardly ever cried, but my face was wet. What part of my appearance announced me as a tramp? How could I prevent it? Each day negative labels seemed to find me despite my great need to be pure. Did the boy think I was a hussy, that I had teased him, that I had run away on purpose to further humiliate him? I missed the possibility of his presence even as I felt sorry that he didn't get time away on the horse his mother had furiously saddled, missed him because I realized anew that despite living in a large family, if not for Duchess, I was alone.

Worse, it felt like I had lost an important fight because I was certain his mother had turned to him and said triumphantly, "See, I told you she was up to no good."

Catherine Magdalena

The Cowboy and His Horse

I peeked out from behind the shrouds of denial today and faced my newly inherited 1969 Ford F250. I sat for a time and observed it parked there, patient like a tethered horse. It seemed animate, like it would spring to life at any moment. This urged me to get started, it had already been waiting two weeks since we made the journey together across state lines and the Cascade Mountain range.

I moved closer to the truck and simply got started, became embroiled in a process that conjured up memories of which I was not prepared. There were rays of light mixed with the darkness of reality and its consequences. Dad brought home this truck brand new, factory standard. I remember his sense of pride and renewed hope. It was a vessel for his rekindled passion for life, he was ready to pick up the pieces after mom's young death and move on. He and my brother and I were still a family and there was a future after all. I was nine. I am now thirty-nine.

I realize now what a pragmatic choice the truck was. The truck was his companion; he took care of it like a good cowboy takes care of his horse. It served him well all those years on the farm, hauling livestock, a one and a half ton fuel tank for the growing and harvest seasons, and everything else a family farm demands. No one ever questioned its usefulness and we could always depend on it. However, just as the last decade of Dad's own life, the truck too got abandoned, parked in the machine shed under nesting pigeons and decomposing straw. When I found the truck after Dad's death, the tires were flat, the bed overflowed with mature Milwaukee's Best beer cans, mismatched hubcaps and rusty oil cans. Drifting loess from plowed fields and past harvests infiltrated every crevice. The truck had outlived him but it was questionable if it could actually overcome it's long period of neglect, and today I see how my over-enthusiastic optimism disabled all rational judgment. When I told my brother I was taking the truck, I was met with no opposition.

Dad drank...a lot... and inevitably lost his license eight years before his death. This loss tugs at my heart, Dad stripped of this basic right, the cowboy without his horse. He never really got that drinking only perpetuates a whole new level of pain. I have no desire to ever witness that kind of show again in my lifetime.

As I cleaned and hauled garbage out, my idealism and nostalgia dampened. The grime, grease and mouse feces were overwhelming. There was spilled Copenhagen spit baked on the dash, equally as difficult to move as my father's obstinate addiction and inflexible mentality; the layers of grease and compacted dirt, unbelievable. I think about the nationally recognized Palouse of eastern Washington and northern Idaho, whose fertile farm ground's higher purpose really is to grow world class wheat and life altering vegetables, not lose its fertility among the death and decay of the floorboards and dash of my newly acquired possession. Most people would have taken one look at this truck's condition and walked away to call the local junkyard. But I gave it not a second thought and drove it 500 miles across the states of Idaho and Washington. No radio, no latex gloves, just a farm upbringing that gifted me the grit to take on this project. Ironically enough, underneath the muck, the interior is in mint condition. The vintage character begins to beam as the decay is stripped away, like the wisdom of an old growth forest and the patina of an aging farmhouse. This unveiling is similar to the unblocking of energy as when clouds part and the sun radiates its life giving warmth, I feel one with this same kind of healing energy.

The truck is a totem of my father's astonishing constitution, his ability to endure the pain of years of self sabotage and neglect. Working to save the truck is an analogy of what I could have done for Dad had he allowed it. I can't change the past or the guilty feelings of personal responsibility. Attempts to save my dad jeopardized my own family and I know the choices I made then are ones I would still choose now. I suddenly feel my throat constrict as I realize that the option to save him is gone forever. His death is real now and with it comes relief but intense grief, even more so that he AND my mom are gone from me forever. I am able to keep going with the focus that what I can do is honor his truck because I can save it.

After a truck cleaning frenzy, I drove to my 13-year old son's counseling appointment, another emotionally uplifting incident where he and I get to face the fact that we might not ever reach each other and I tell him that I am not the enemy. This is as overwhelming and deep as the other emotional issues of the day but I reluctantly go anyway. After the appointment, we walk back to the truck, get in and close the doors. We look at each other and say slowly, in unison, "what is that smell?" The odor is so strong we both gag and then laugh hysterically; my son's face lightens and probes for answers. It's quickly obvious that my cleaning skills didn't take into account the effect of heat on the newly exposed decade old compounds created from cleaning. Why do I choose to put my energy into such a gross inanimate object, I wonder? I then see an immediate benefit from taking on this project because I become aware that it takes this level of intensity in a situation for my son and I to reach each other. I could see this as comedy or tragedy, nonetheless, something positive just happened and I hope this twisted irony makes my dad smile. And then I wonder what any one I know and admire do given the same inheritance? Run fast, I speculate. I know this must be making my dad laugh. I laugh, hysterically at this crazy turn of events of the day.

My son and I tolerate the smell, we do need to get home tonight and this is our ride. We are both silently relieved about enduring this odor as it pulls us out of our heads from the counseling session and we connect through this common struggle.

We drive on through the stench to pick up his sister at dance class. I know what my daughter's reaction will be. She is eleven and completely critical of me of course; her adolescent, developmentally appropriate right. I am tolerant because I know she lives in fear that she will be just like me. She gets in the truck and I hear, "Mom! Why can't we drive something normal!" However, she surprises me and doesn't say anything more about the truck, only expresses enthusiasm about her dance class. I appreciate her bouncy spirit. My son and I exchange a gaze of common understanding.

On our drive home, my thoughts also ponder about these two younger children of mine and their experience of their grandfather; his drunken ranting, unpredictable moods, and the disorderly farmhouse and outbuildings. They never knew the brilliant and beautiful soul that their two older siblings and I understood and loved. They never romped in the hay barn or played cow rodeo, never rode a motorcycle through the stubble fields, never saw the sun set across the canyon. They never knew that every item on the farm had a place and nothing was ever broken for long. They were born during that last decade of advanced disease, neglect and abandonment.

They haven't discussed what they think about all of this, the few times they've seen his life's disorder and then his death, and now my concentrated efforts to not only unearth what probably appears to be a throwaway farm truck but what remains of the farm in general. I imagine they only know relief that some of this is over, that their mother's worry and grief can eventually subside.

My intuition about the Ford were right, so far it runs great; I mean we made it 500 miles across the states of northern Idaho and Washington on bald tires and an oil change. Air flow will help to squelch the smell, like Dad used to say, "don't worry about the little things, just load the wagon." I guess that means life goes on and you gotta keep moving; there's things to do, people to see, money to make.

Cleaning up the truck is like cleaning up the past and the good times are visible and appreciated because of it. My childhood was dotted with crazy and tragic happenings but now I see the richness of insight and how I am a better human because of it. Behind the wheel, I feel Dad's spirit and the misunderstandings and mishaps throughout our lives have lost their significance. Death has released us, I see that his soul is clear now, no longer fogged with pain and addiction. The truck is an awakened being; I feel good I was able to facilitate its renewed integrity to carry on its usefulness.

I am both the Palouse of northern Idaho and the west coast of Washington, the diversity and richness of this brings my soul to its knees; I've been given a divine gift. I truly am blessed.

Jeremiah Horrigan

In the Morning Kitchen

My grandmother would sit across from me at the small, flour-dusted kitchen table, coffee cup in her right hand, cigarette in her left and tilt her head to one side as she watched me eat the bread we'd just made together.

"How is it?" she'd ask.

I'd like to report that I'd told her the truth – that I'd said it was the best bread I'd ever eaten in my life. That making bread with her was even better than Saturday morning cartoons. And that I loved her for treating me like a grown-up and not just a little kid.

But I was just a little kid, so all I said was "Good."

She would smile when she heard me say that. But then, memory tells me she smiled at me all the time. I knew at some deep-down unspoken level that I was her favorite. I can only hope that she knew she was mine.

I took a lot for granted back then, including those smiles. Like any kid, I thought they'd last forever. But soon we had moved away and I saw her only on infrequent visits home and then, when I was ten years older, away at college, she was gone. I didn't even come home to see her buried.

It's not her voice that sometimes taunts me with this shameful knowledge; it's my own.

Even now, some forty years on, she makes no demands on me from the grave, as the dead sometimes do. She asks for no explanation, demands no penance. I'm sure she knows I'll go to my own grave not understanding why I never said a final good-bye.

CONTRIBUTORS

ANN MARIE BYRD, Ph.D., has published in *America in WWII, Flashquake, Literary Mama, Long Story Short, Gloom Cupboard, Lost Magazine, Puffin Circus, Flashlight Memories Anthology, The Harsh and the Heart Anthology*, and others. A Pushcart Prize nominee, she is an editorial assistant with *Fiction Fix*, the University of North Florida's literary magazine. She resides in Jacksonville with her husband and son.

JANET YOUNGBLOOD, the subject of Ann Marie Byrd's piece, is a feisty 93-year old who shared her story, through conversations, of being one of the first women to enter the newly created Women's Army Auxiliary Corps in 1942.

TIFFANY JOY BUTLER is a multimedia artist, having studied electronic arts, painting, and writing at Alfred University. She is now primarily focused on writing memoirs and screenplays. Tiffany Joy continues to draw, paint, and create humorous animations. She currently resides in Brooklyn, New York.

CATHLEEN CALBERT's work has appeared in many publications, including *Ms. Magazine, The New York Times*, and *The Paris Review*. She is the author of three books of poetry: *Lessons in Space* (University of Florida Press), *Bad Judgment* (Sarabande Books), and *Sleeping with a Famous Poet* (C.W. Books). A collection of short fiction, *The Ten Worst Human Fears*, is forthcoming from Rooster Hill Press.

MARTHA CLARKSON manages corporate workplace design in Seattle. Her poetry and fiction can be found in *Monkeybicycle6, Clackamas Literary Review, descant, Seattle Review, Portland Review, elimae*, and *Nimrod*. She is a recipient of a Washington State Poets William Stafford prize 2005, a Pushcart Nomination, and is listed under "Notable Stories," Best American Non-Required Reading for 2007 and 2009.

THERESA CORBIN was born and raised in a small town outside of New Orleans, Louisiana and is from a long line of creoles, who live for and love and laugh with sarcasm and spice. She attended Louisiana State University, where she was torn between her home in Slidell, and her new life at school two hours away from her mother who was dying of cancer. At LSU while healing from the loss of her mother Theresa plunged herself into learning everything she could about anything she wasn't majoring in. That's when she stumbled upon Islam. A month after her conversion her father suffered a catastrophic heart attack and passed away. Theresa then took a hiatus from school to figure out how to deal with the loneliness of being an orphan, and to learn who she would be as a Muslim. She married and moved to

Mobile, AL and settled into her new community as an active member, teacher, and foster parent. Theresa is now back in school at The University of South Alabama working toward interfaith understanding and cooperation through her writing.

MADELINE DAVIS was born in 1940 in Buffalo, NY, and received BA, MA & MLS from University of Buffalo. She is a political activist, singer, songwriter, poet, memoirist, librarian (33 years), historian, quilter, and breed dog rescuer. Madeline lives with her wife, five cats and our elderly keeshond.

FRANCIS DICLEMENTE is the author of *Outskirts of Intimacy*, a poetry chapbook published by Flutter Press. He lives in Syracuse, New York, where he works as a video producer. In his spare time, he writes and takes photographs.

KENT H. DIXON has published in all genres, predominantly fiction and nonfiction, most notably in *Georgia Review, Iowa Review, TriQuarterly, Antioch Review, Kansas Quarterly, Gettysburg Review, Energy Review, Shenandoah,* and *The American Prospect.* He's won awards and contests—Ohio Arts Council grants, Pushcart nominations, Story Magazine's Love Story competition, Finalist and Semi-finalist here and there. He lives in Springfield, Ohio, where he teaches literature and creative writing at Wittenberg University, and makes the occasional journalistic foray into the likes of jail ("48 Hours in the County Jail," *Grand Tour*). Of late, he's into white water kayaking, though in fact he's a pretty fearful and cautious guy.

CATHY CRENSHAW DOHENY is a native of Charlotte, North Carolina. She holds a Bachelor of Music degree in Vocal Performance from the University of North Carolina School of the Arts and has sung with numerous regional opera companies. Equally at home in the literary world, her writing focuses on the arts, parenting and medical topics. She is the Winner of the Kaixin Inaugural Writing Competition, and Runner-Up in the Southwestern Writers International Writing Competition. A freelance journalist, Cathy's work has been published by *Adoption Today Magazine, Faith and Family Magazine, Liver Health Today,* and *Neurology Now.* She is currently a contributing writer for *Asian Fortune News* and *The Charlotte Observer's University City Magazine.* Her creative nonfiction pieces have been published in numerous anthologies, including *A Cup of Comfort for Mothers, Pets Across America 2* and *Root Exposure - New Voices in Literature.* Cathy is the "Famous Operas" contributing writer for *The Daily Book of Classical Music* (Walter Foster Publishing 2010). In 2011, she also had the honor of having her work published in the *Adoption Fact Book* (National Council for Adoption). She lives with her husband, Kevin, six-year-old daughter, Jade, and their three dogs and two cats in Charlotte, NC.

PAUL DRAGAVON recently passed. He was born and raised in northern Minnesota, in a town called Tower, where his story took place. He often wrote fictional stories based on real life experiences including various thoughts and memos to his grandchildren. Paul also wrote poetry and political essays and lived in California.

JARED DURAN is a student of creative writing at Glendale Community College, a member of *The Traveler* literary magazine staff, and, above all, a writer. He lives with his fiancée in Phoenix, Arizona with her children, three cats, and a dog.

ADINA FERGUSON is a writer of many genres. Born, raised and resident of Washington, DC she holds a BA in English Language and Literature from University of Maryland-College Park, where she also works doing nothing in relation to her passion for words. In recent years, Adina has been published in media outlets including *The Starting Five, DC Metro Sports* and University of Maryland's daily newspaper, *The Diamondback.*

MAUREEN TOLMAN FLANNERY's latest book is *Tunnel into Morning.* Other volumes of her work include *Destiny Whispers to the Beloved, Ancestors in the Landscape,* and *Secret of the Rising up.* Maureen was raised on a Wyoming sheep ranch and moved, with her actor husband Dan, to Chicago where they raised their four children. Her poems have appeared in fifty anthologies and over a hundred literary reviews, including *Birmingham Poetry Review, Xavier Review, Calyx, Pedestal, Atlanta Review, Out of Line, and North American Review, Poetry East,* and *Santa Fe Literary Review.*

RENNY MURPHY GOLDEN is a Poetry Editor with Voices From the American Land Press, Placitas, New Mexico and she is on the Advisory Board for the *Malpais Review.* She is a Professor Emerita from Northeastern Illinois University. Her latest book of poetry, *Blood Desert: Witnesses 1820-1880* (University of New Mexico Press) won the WILLA Literary Award for 2011. Her book of poems *Benedicite* was a Finalist for White Pine Press' Poetry Prize 2010. Golden's book of poetry *The Hour of the Furnaces* was nominated for a National Book Award in 2000. Her book *War on the Family: Imprisoned Mothers and the Families They Left Behind* (Routledge, 2005) was a Finalist for the C Wright Mills Award. *Disposable Children: America's Child Welfare System* (Wadsworth Publishers) was nominated for the American Criminological Association's Hindelang Award and Delta Kappa Gamma Society's Educator's Award. She co-authored *Oscar Romero,* (Orbis, 2000) now in its fifth printing. *The Hour of the Poor, the Hour of Women* (Crossroads Publishing), won Crossroads Women's Studies Award; and *Sanctuary: the New Underground Railroad,* with Michael McConnell, (Orbis,

1986) received a Gustavus Meyer Human Rights Award from the University of Alabama.

JOAN GOODREAU's stories, articles and poems have appeared in such publications as *Fiddler Head, Dalhousie Review, Bloodroot Literary Magazine, Ottawa Poetry Journal, Plus Women's Magazine, Watershed Literary Magazine, The Word Magazine, The Derelict Voice, The 99 Words Collection, Flashquake*, and *Ahoy*. She recently completed a Hedgebrook residency where she worked on a memoir, *The Longest Year*, about her son with autism. She has been a Special Education teacher and program specialist. A native Californian, she lived in England and Canada and now resides in Chico, California.

KEVIN HEATH holds a Ph.D. in creative writing from the University of Cincinnati. He recently won the *Tusculum Review* prize in fiction for a co-authored collection of genre-X called *29 Pieces From The Lost Book of Hawkwoman*. He lives in Cedarville OH with his wife and three children.

ERICA HERD is a New Jersey-based freelance writer and full-time legal secretary, former English teacher, cabaret artist and member of a New York City sketch comedy troupe. Her poetry was published by Little Episodes in the U.K. in October 2010. She writes a blog on *Open Salon* and is currently working on a one-woman show about her mom who suffers from Alzheimer's disease. She is a native New Yorker who grew up in Jackson Heights, Queens and Hollywood, California.

JANE HERTENSTEIN lives in Chicago where she cooks, writes, and blogs at http://www.memoirouswrite.blogspot.com. Previous work has appeared in: *Hunger Mountain, Rosebud, Word Riot, Flashquake, Steam Ticket, The Write Room, Frostwriting, Cantaraville, Fiction Fix, Six Minute Magazine*, and *Tonopah Review*.

JEREMIAH HORRIGAN is a former Knight of the Altar from South Buffalo, NY, and is old enough to remember ducking-and-covering from the threat of nukes. He defended Santa Claus until the age of ten, hated playing sports, attended Fordham U, dropped out, got political, got arrested, got tried, got convicted, sentenced and released for crimes against the draft. Jeremiah has been a housepainter, cab driver, idiot, newspaper reporter, and freelance writer (Sports Illustrated, The New York Times, Negligent Mother Magazine). As a daily reporter for Middletown Times Herald-Record, he has written scads of other people's stories over some twenty years, won some awards, and made discoveries large and small along the way. Jeremiah is a husband to Patty, and a father to Grady and Annie.

CHANTAL JULES was born in Marseille, France on May 29th 1976 and immigrated to the US when she was a few years old. In 2007, the father of her children and soul mate was killed on the streets of Chicago. "Stilettos" was written six months after his death. After four years of deep mourning she has finally emerged a bit stronger, a bit more confident, yet still not sure what the future holds for her and her family. Chantal lives in Joliet, Illinois with her daughter Mariah, and sons Antonio and Angelo.

MARTY KINGSBURY is a poet, novelist, and instructor of English at the Urban College of Boston. She is currently working on a novel about street dogs in South America called *Rescuing Oricito*.

MARILYN JUNE JANSON, M.S.Ed., is the author of *Recipe For Rage*, a suspense novel, and *Tommy Jenkins: First Teleported Kid*, a children's chapter book.

CHARLOTTE JONES writes poetry, short stories and novels in Houston, Texas.

JACQUELINE M. KOINER The author grew up in Queens, NY to father, author and playwright Richard B. Koiner and mother artist and homemaker Jacqueline M. Koiner, senior. She is an alumnus of University of Phoenix and currently enrolled in Walden University where she is completing her Master's of Mental Health Counseling. She currently lives with her partner of ten years in Farmville, Virginia.

MARYLEE MACDONALD's fiction has appeared in *StoryQuarterly*, *Bellevue Literary Review*, *American Literary Review*, *North Atlantic Review*, *Ruminate*, and others.

CATHERINE MAGDALENA grew up in northern Idaho on a 4th generation family farm, at the eastern edge of The Palouse. She has been migrating west since reaching adulthood from Moscow, Idaho to Seattle. She now resides in Portland, Oregon and works in property management in downtown Portland. Catherine has worked in many capacities of property management and social services that lend to her diverse perspectives of human behavior and social patterns. She has four children who are now grown and blazing their own trails. Catherine sees the beauty in tragedy and chooses to write about the positive born out of adversity. She plans to take this time without children to publish her writing.

STEPHANIE MILLETT was born in Ft. Wayne, Indiana, and moved to St. George, Utah, at the age of 12 where she still lives today. She is the mother of three boys. She has worked as a medical transcriptionist for ten years. She is currently working on her BS degree in English Professional and Technical Writing at Dixie State College. Stephanie is a cancer survivor, diagnosed with leukemia in 1999, and she has been in remission since 2000. After the death of her eldest son in 2009, she found her passion in writing as an outlet of personal expression and her voice to the world.

CHRISTINE MINTER is from Atlanta and is a retired schoolteacher living in Stone Mountain, Georgia.

ANN MINTZ has had six careers and has lived in seven cities, if you count Philadelphia twice. She intends to stay in Philadelphia this time, where she lives with her husband and two rescued dogs.

SHERYL L. NELMS is from Marysville, Kansas. She graduated from South Dakota State University with a B.S. in Family Relations and Child Development. She has had over 5,000 poems, stories and articles published. Some of the magazines, anthologies and textbooks that have used her work are: *Readers Digest, Modern Maturity, Kaleidoscope, Capper's, Grit, Country Woman, Poetry Now, Confrontation, Strings, This Delicious Day, The American Anthology* and *Men Freeing Men*. Fourteen collections of her poetry have been published. They are: *Their Combs Turn Red In The Spring, The Oketo Yahoos, Strawberries and Rhubarb, Land of the Blue Paloverde, Friday Night Desperate, Technology & Rural America, Aunt Emma Collected T eeth, Howling At the Gibbous Moon, Greatest Hits 1978-2003, The Stalking Spirits, Secrets of the Wind, Can You Imagine Oral Sex, A Collection of Poems and Bluebonnets, Boots* and *Buffalo Bones*. She was the editor of *Oakwood* and *Crawford's Chronicles*; and contributing editor to *Byline*, and *Streets*. She has been a staff writer for several newspapers and magazines. She is currently the fiction/non-fiction editor of *The Pen Woman Magazine*, the national magazine of the National League of American Pen Women. She makes a living as an insurance agent. Sheryl is also a painter, a weaver and an old dirt biker.

NANCY OWEN NELSON has published articles, poems and creative nonfiction, and has edited three books. A college professor and formerly Assistant Director of the Hassayampa Institute, she is currently teaching a workshop in memoir for Springfed Arts in Detroit, MI.

NANCY NICOL attended Friends Seminary in Manhattan for eleven years where art and creative writing were basic in her education. She graduated from Harvard Graduate School of Education and is a marriage and family therapist as well as an artist with a gallery in Wellfleet, MA. Her motto, Time is Everything, is reflected in a daily practice of meditation, journal-writing and painting in the studio. She self-published a memoir cookbook *Atwood*

Farm Kitchen Secrets, and currently working on her novel, *The Disengagement of Ms. Fiona Frost*.

KATHLEEN O'BRIEN teaches 11th and 12th grade English in Reno, Nevada. Earlier work appeared in the anthology *A Waist is a Terrible Thing to Mind* published by The Real Women Project.

HAL O'LEARY is an eighty-six-year-old Secular Humanist who, having spent his life in the theatre, believes that it only through the arts, poetry in particular, that one is afforded an occasional glimpse into the otherwise incomprehensible. Hal is the recipient of an Honorary Doctor of Humane Letters degree from West Liberty University.

HELEN PEPPE is a writer and nature photographer. The former editor of *Eastern Equerry* and *Wordplay Magazine*, her short stories, articles, and photographs have appeared in anthologies and magazines, including *Practical Horseman, Equus, American Trakehner, Arabian Horse Times, Dog Fancy, Dog World, Dressage Today, Equine Journal, The Horse, Horse Journal Quarterly, Lynx Eye, Mused Literary Review* and *Cats Magazine*. Several of her short stories and photographs appear in textbooks and educational media. Helen is the author of the limited edition *Live on Stage: A History of the State Theater* and creator of the *Maine Stable Guide*, published between 1995 and 2005. Helen's story, "Nomenclature" placed first in the Word Worth 2009 Essay and Fiction Contest, and her story "Food that Bites" placed first in The Starving Writer Literary contest, May 2010; "Walk On" placed first in that same contest August 2010. "Out of Sync," a story on precocious puberty, was the feature in June 2010 The Good Men Project; "The Starting Line" will appear in anthology *PaniK: Candid Stories of Life Altering Experiences Surrounding Pregnancy*; "Where's Margaret?" will appear in Pop Fic Review. Her essay "The American Eagle" is one of seven finalists in the 2011 Annie Dillard Creative Nonfiction Award and her essay "The Bird that Cries with Grief" is a finalist in the 2011 Maine Literary Awards.

GABRIJEL SAVIC RA is a multimedia artist, poet and theorist. He has published two books of poetry and his work appears in various collections of poetry, short stories and art magazines. As an artist he has exhibited worldwide.

MARIAN RAPOPORT is in her sixties who lives with a partner and a rescue dog in the woods outside a small town in southern Vermont. She writes when the muse comes to her and for that she is grateful.

ANJIE SEEWER REYNOLDS' work has been published in *The Christian Science Monitor, The Sun, The Writer's Workshop Review, Drunken Boat, The*

Dos Passos Review, Chronogram, and *Underwired*; her essays have also aired on KQED, San Francisco's NPR affiliate. She currently lives in Ashland, Oregon, with her favorite dentist and their two children.

MOLLY RIVKIN was raised near the small town of Bonners Ferry, Idaho and grew up playing in the woods, hiking, biking, snowboarding, camping, and rebelling against her 'hippie' parents. She attended the University of Idaho for her first year of college, joined a sorority, and took her first Gender Studies class. After that she transferred to the University of Montana and dedicated the rest of her college career to Liberal Studies, Gender Studies, Spanish, snowboarding, and women's rugby. She has since tried her hand at wildland firefighting, ski bumming, adventuring to Maine, and waitressing and her next great adventure will be joining the Peace Corps leaving for Ukraine in March, 2012.

MARK SABA is the author of two short novels: *The Landscapes of Pater* (The Vineyard Press, New York, 2004) and *Thaddeus Olsen* (in the volume Desperate Remedies, Apis Books, London, 2008). His stories, poems, and essays have appeared in various literary magazines and anthologies. He is also a painter, and works as a medical illustrator and graphic designer at Yale University. See www.marksabawriter.com.

VENETIA SJOGREN is a fifty-three year old disabled homo sapien, fem, grandmother, of mixed cultural heritage, borderline atheist, humanist, non-tribalist, apolitical who attempts to write words of thunder when she is not busy looking for "earn the gruel contract jobs."

ALAN L. STEINBERG works at SUNY Potsdam and over the years has published fiction, poetry, and drama, including *Cry of the Leopard* (St. Martin's Press), *Fathering* (Sarasota Poetry Press), and *The Road to Corinth* (Players Press).

TERRY MEYER STONE lives on a vineyard in Western Canada with her husband, two of four children, three dogs, and three cats. She writes for *Wine Trails Magazine* and was a former TV Host, entrepreneur and Miss Canada1975.

FRAN TEMPEL grew up in Montana; she is now married and lives in upstate New York. As a teacher she taught her students to keep personal journals, trying to convince them that everyone's life, not just the rich and famous, is worth documenting.

DEBORAH THOMPSON is an Associate Professor of English at Colorado State University, where she helped to develop the new master's degree in Creative Nonfiction. She has published numerous essays in literary criticism and nonfiction. Her piece "Mishti Kukur," which appeared in *The Iowa Review*, recently won a Pushcart prize. Debby belongs to the Slow Sand Writer's Society, to whose members she is beyond grateful.

APRIL C. THORNTON is a resident of Mobile, AL where she is currently studying as an English Major with a focus on Creative Writing. Her works range from poetry to fiction to creative nonfiction. When she is not focused on her writing she serves as the Director of a Christian Recreation Facility. April's biggest source of joy is spending quality time with her family.

KERRY TRAUTMAN writes at dawn in small-town Ohio. Her poetry and short fiction have appeared in various print and online journals and in the anthologies, *Tuesday Nights at Sam and Andy's Uptown Café* (Westron Press, 2001), and *Mourning Sickness* (Omniarts 2008).

JOE WADE is an eight-year veteran, having spent three years in the army and five years in the navy. Thanks to the efforts of his beloved professors (Mrs. Weaver, Damato-Beamesderfer, Dr. Stumphy, "Trum" and Cockeram) he's turned into a writer who is now attending Brooklyn College as a Scholars student. Joseph's published work can also be found in *A Long Story Short*, and forthcoming in *Grey Sparrow Journal*.

SARAH L. WEBB is a recent graduate of California College of the Arts where she received an M. F. A. in Writing. After living in Mississippi and California for seven years, she is now teaching literature and writing in her hometown of Baton Rouge, Louisiana. In addition to writing nonfiction, Sarah also writes fiction, poetry and drama. She founded the blog S. L. Writes, where she shares insights on growing up as an African American girl raised by a single mother. She has published magazines such as *Konch* and *Symposium 2009*.

JANET AMALIA WEINBERG is a former psychologist, and the editor of an anthology designed to help women feel good about aging, *Still Going Strong; Memoirs, Stories, and Poems About Great Older Women* (Routledge). Her stories and articles have appeared in *Room, Mused, Long Story Short, Wild Violet, West Wind Review, Long Island Woman, Moondance* and elsewhere.

GUINOTTE WISE is the Creative Director at an advertising agency in Kansas City. Educated at Westminster College, University of Arkansas, and Kansas City Art Institute, Wise is a sculptor in welded steel and in words. His literary awards include being semi-finalist for the Nimrod 2010 Katherine Anne Porter Prize for Fiction for "Varga Girl." "Night Train" won both 2nd place winner for Medulla Review 2010 Oblongata Flash Fiction, and Honorable Mention in Oaxaca Film Festival & Literary Awards 2010.

KIRK WISLAND grew up fast on the mean frozen streets of Minneapolis, but following an MFA sojourn at the University of Arizona he now makes his home in the peaceful coastal warmth of southern California. His work has appeared or is forthcoming in *Creative Nonfiction, Paper Darts, The Diagram, Phoebe, the Normal School,* and *Fiction on a Stick.*

ABOUT THE EDITOR

CoCo Harris lives for story.

Her story began in Atlanta, GA, and has traversed the Nation's capital, West Africa, Seattle, WA, Louisville, KY, Coastal Georgia, and the Susquehanna Valley. Though she now lives in central PA, CoCo is particularly at home anywhere sun and surf meet.

She earned a B.S. in Electrical Engineering at Howard University, did graduate work in African Studies, and began her Intellectual Property Law career working for the Patent and Trademark Office while becoming a wife and a mother of three daughters. She later entered the US Patent Bar becoming a patent law professional representing individuals, firms, and corporations in the US and abroad.

CoCo received her Master of Fine Arts in Writing in Fiction from Spalding University, and is a Zora Neale Hurston/Richard Wright Foundation alumna. As a lifetime diarist, she is drawn to personal narratives. For years she has guided others with crafting personal narratives through creative writing workshops and various memoir projects.

CoCo Harris is constantly exploring the notion of how we tell the stories of our lives.